The Australian
FISHERMAN'S
COMPANION

Harold Vaughan

HERRON
book distributors Pty Ltd

This edition distributed by Herron Books, Qld
Published in Australia by
New Holland Publishers (Australia) Pty Ltd
Sydney • Auckland • London • Cape Town
1/66 Gibbes Street Chatswood NSW 2067 Australia
218 Lake Road Northcote Auckland New Zealand
86 Edgware Road London W2 2EA United Kingdom
80 McKenzie Street Cape Town 8001 South Africa

First published by Lansdowne Press 1982
Revised edition 1984
Reprinted 1985, 1986, 1987, 1989
Reprinted by Ure Smith Press 1991, 1992
Reprinted by Lansdowne Publishing Pty Ltd 1994, 1995, 1996, 1997,
1998, 1999
Reprinted by New Holland Publishers (Australia) Pty Ltd 2001, 2008,
2009, 2011

1 2 3 4 5 6 7 8

A CiP record of this title is available from the National Library of
Australia

ISBN 9781864367683

Typeset in Australia by Pavilion Press Set
Printed in China by Toppan Printing Co.

CONTENTS

INTRODUCTION

Most illustrated books of fishes group the fish in families, for example, cod or perch. Other books illustrate the fish and list them alphabetically under their common names.

This means that to identify a fish, one needs to know something about its family background, or proceed to thumb right through the book.

This handbook is different. All 240 species, common to Australian waters, listed here have been grouped into ten easy to follow sections.

To identify a certain fish, all one has to do is determine:
a) **Has the fish got scales?**
   If the answer is No look at Section 1   (P.14)
   If the answer is Yes proceed to the next question.
b) **Is it a flat fish like a flounder or a flathead?**
   If the answer is Yes look at Section 2   (P.34)
   If the answer is No
c) **Determine the shape of its fin tail and look up the appropriate section.**

About Tail Fins

A few fish are borderline cases and it could be that a fish with a forked tail may be in our deep forked section, whereas it could reasonably be assumed to be in the moderate forked section. This only happens on odd occasions and means that in such borderline cases both sections may have to be looked up.

Notwithstanding, we know of no better way the average fisherman has of determining WHAT FISH IS THAT?

EXPLANATORY NOTES

In the following pages you will find a number of ways to rig your line. Each rig is numbered and they co-ordinate with the identification section.

There are no hard and fast rules, but these are proven rigs and accepted by most fishermen as being effective for a variety of conditions. Make minor changes if you feel that conditions warrant them. A 3kg (7lb) fish caught on sand in a few metres of water may only require a 6kg (13lb) line to play and haul it aboard, whereas the same fish caught near oyster-covered rocks or coral will require a line considerably heavier. Always remember that when all factors are equal the angler with the light line will have more action. Avoid using a heavy sinker when a lighter one will do. A floating bait near the bottom is better than one anchored or lying still in the mud or sand. Use the current and tide to assist in making your bait more attractive to the fish.

When anchored in a strong flow, rigs no. 4 and no. 15 with a two metre trace are excellent. Bait the hook and hold the sinker in your hand while you play out at least twice the amount of line required to reach the bottom. Now let the sinker slide down the line and you have an attractive bait waving about near the bottom. The size of the sinker to be used is a matter of the tide flow, current or drift and for that reason is not mentioned.

Many rock-dwellers, such as the groper, will rise to a bait, then dive for a cave or rock crevice where it will wedge itself and defy any amount of tugging. Obviously, a heavy line, far in excess of what fish's size suggests, is necessary to land it.

Good knots are essential to successful fishing and they must be carefully formed by ensuring that the turns and pass-throughs are correct and that there is no serious necking down where the line enters and crosses.

Nylon line usually sets better if the ends are placed in the mouth for a few seconds before knotting.

Here are some of the most useful knots:

JOINING LINES

The blood knot is by far the best knot ever devised for joining nylon lines. Fine line, say under 6kg (14lb) breaking strain, should be tied with four turns each side.

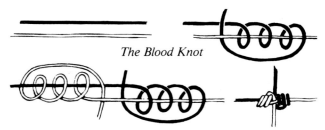

The Blood Knot

TYING TO A RING OR SWIVEL

The three-turn half blood knot is regarded as the strongest and best for tying nylon line to a wire ring. Take three turns and clinch the free end by passing it back through the ring and then laid along the bight of the line, then doubled back in a big loop and the free end is passed around the two strands and through the loop twice, and pulled tight.

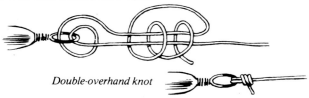

Double-overhand knot

SNOODING A HOOK TO A LINE

1. The end is laid along the shank of the hook and a loop is formed. This loop should be half as long again as the hook, so that it may be slipped over it a number of times.
2. The lower strand of the loop is now picked up and carried up over the shank, the bend of the hook passing through it in the process.

3. Before the manoeuvre can be repeated wind the same strand in another turn around the shank.
4. Five, six or more turns may be wound on in this manner.

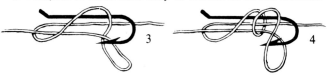

5. and **6.** The snood is closed by pulling back the line to take up the loop.

RIGGING YOUR LINE

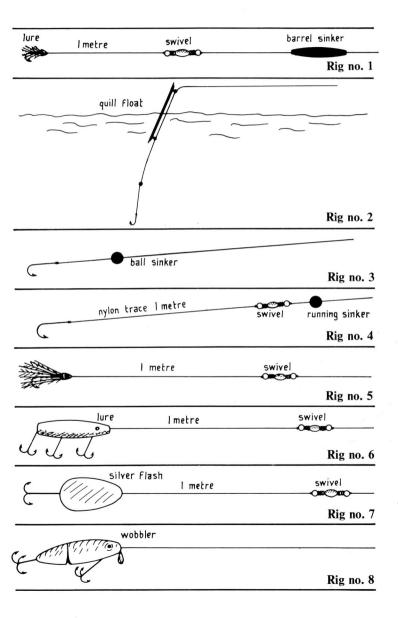

lure   1 metre   swivel   barrel sinker

Rig no. 1

quill float

Rig no. 2

ball sinker

Rig no. 3

nylon trace 1 metre   swivel   running sinker

Rig no. 4

1 metre   swivel

Rig no. 5

lure   1 metre   swivel

Rig no. 6

silver flash   1 metre   swivel

Rig no. 7

wobbler

Rig no. 8

9

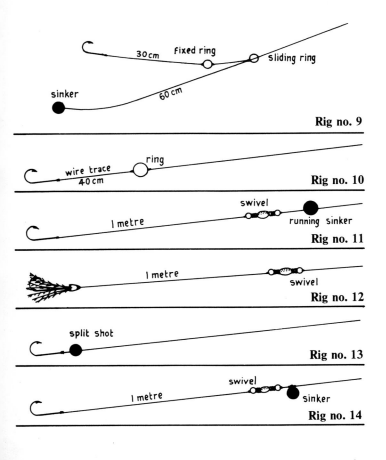

30cm   fixed ring

sliding ring

sinker

60 cm

Rig no. 9

wire trace   ring

40 cm

Rig no. 10

swivel

1 metre

running sinker

Rig no. 11

1 metre

swivel

Rig no. 12

split shot

Rig no. 13

swivel

1 metre

sinker

Rig no. 14

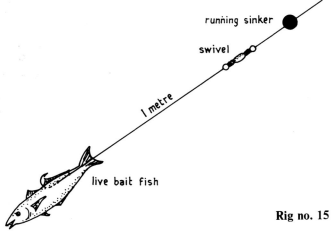

running sinker

swivel

1 metre

live bait fish

Rig no. 15

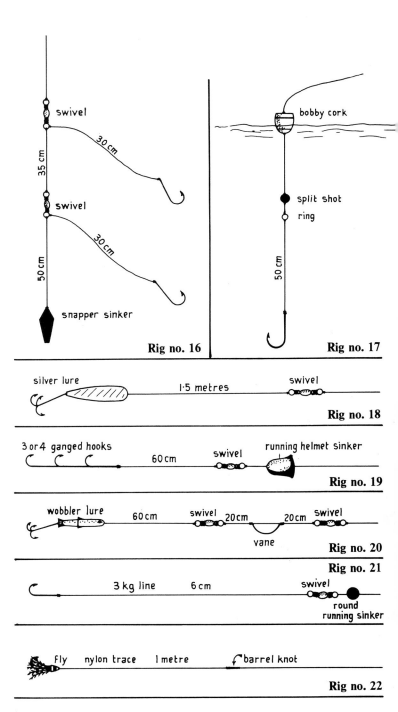

swivel

30 cm

35 cm

swivel

30 cm

50 cm

snapper sinker

Rig no. 16

bobby cork

split shot

ring

50 cm

Rig no. 17

silver lure

1·5 metres

swivel

Rig no. 18

3 or 4 ganged hooks

60 cm

swivel

running helmet sinker

Rig no. 19

wobbler lure

60 cm

swivel 20 cm

20 cm swivel

vane

Rig no. 20

Rig no. 21

3 kg line

6 cm

swivel

round
running sinker

fly   nylon trace   1 metre   barrel knot

Rig no. 22

11

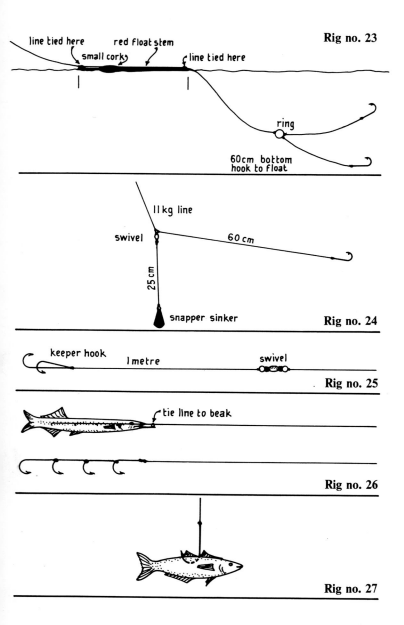

Rig no. 23

line tied here

red float stem

small cork

line tied here

ring

60cm bottom hook to float

11 kg line

swivel

60 cm

25 cm

snapper sinker

Rig no. 24

keeper hook

1 metre

swivel

Rig no. 25

tie line to beak

Rig no. 26

Rig no. 27

12

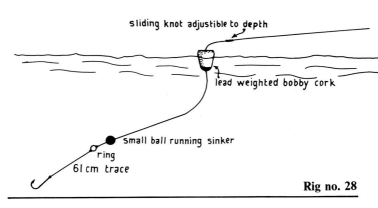

sliding knot adjustible to depth

lead weighted bobby cork

small ball running sinker

ring

61 cm trace

Rig no. 28

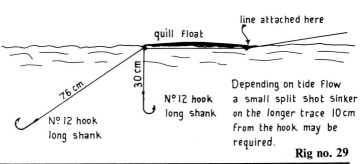

line attached here

quill float

30 cm

76 cm

Nº 12 hook long shank

Nº 12 hook long shank

Depending on tide flow a small split shot sinker on the longer trace 10 cm from the hook may be required.

Rig no. 29

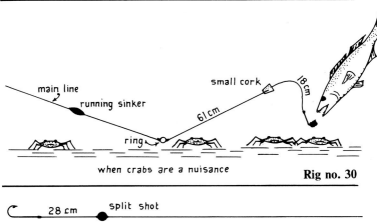

main line

running sinker

small cork

18 cm

61 cm

ring

when crabs are a nuisance

Rig no. 30

28 cm   split shot

Rig no. 31

13

CHAPTER ONE

Fish without Scales

LEATHERJACKET, BRIDLED
Acanthaluteres spilomelanurus

Body elongate and not as deep as other species of leatherjacket. Bridled leatherjacket has a small mouth with sharp teeth. The dorsal spine consists of a membrane and four spines, situated above the eyes. The tail fin is rounded and the body is covered in a rough multi-coloured jacket, generally green above with a number of blue spots. A blue line edged in black from below the mouth to the eye and continuing towards the tail is a characteristic marking.

Bridled leatherjacket makes good eating.

HABITAT AND GROWTH
Found in close offshore waters to a depth of 35 m (115 ft) off New South Wales, Victoria, Tasmania and South Australia. A reef species which grows to 20 cm (8 in).

FISHING
Not a fussy eater, it will take any fish bait, prawn, etc. Use a no. 10 hook with a light wire trace to a 5 kg (11 lb) line and rig no. 4. Fish the bottom.

LEATHERJACKET, CHINAMAN
Nelusetta ayraudi
Also called Yellow Leatherjacket.

This is the largest of our leatherjacket species. As the name implies, it is yellow with bright yellow fins.

The flesh is excellent and is often sold as butterfish.

HABITAT AND GROWTH
Particularly plentiful some years ago, Chinaman leatherjacket became a real nuisance to deep-sea fishermen as they often bit the line off just below the surface with their very sharp teeth. Also occurs in estuaries around the southern half of the country, in rock and sand. Estuary size is usually less than 25 cm (10 in).

FISHING

If they are plentiful, you can sometimes entice the fish to the surface by holding the head or gut of a fish in the water with one hand. You can then pluck them out and into the boat with the other. They are slow-moving and their leather jacket makes them easy to handle. They are easy to clean and skin by cutting behind the head spear down to the gut sack. By pulling the head down, the gut sack will come away with the head, leaving the fish ready for skinning. Pull the skin back to the tail. Will eat almost anything, but you need a wire trace or a long shanked 1/0 hook. Use rig no. 11.

LEATHERJACKET, FAN-BELLIED

Monacanthus chinensis

Also known as a Centreboard Jacket.

A particularly deep-bodied fish of brownish-green colouring with irregular dark blotches. Characteristic features are the over-developed stomach flap and the delicately lined dorsal and anal fins.

Like all leatherjackets the flesh is firm and good eating although they are only small.

HABITAT AND GROWTH

Fan-bellied leatherjacket has a wide range and is known to extend into the Torres Straits. It is common in the rivers and estuaries in most States where it attains a growth of 25 cm (10 in).

FISHING

Usually caught with a luderick rig using no. 8 or no. 10 hook and a small piece of peeled prawn, around old wharves and jetties.

LEATHERJACKET, FANTAIL

Alutera scripta

Also known as Scribbled Leatherjacket.

This is a very slow-moving species, grey, with the characteristic trigger spike above the eyes and large fan-like tail and fins. A deep, thin body covered by drab, tough, scaleless skin.

A good food fish.

HABITAT AND GROWTH

Often observed and caught around piles and wharves and along rocky river foreshores. They are particularly plentiful around the Sydney area. Grow to only about 500 g (1 lb).

FISHING

Use a luderick rig and a no. 6 hook on rig no. 31. Any usual fish bait, prawn, cunjevoi or squid will do. It is a simple fish to clean

and skin. Cut behind the trigger spike down to the stomach stock. Hold the body in the left hand and with the right hand, pull the head and gut away in one operation. Peel the skin away, starting at the belly flaps.

LEATHERJACKET, HORSE-SHOE

Meuschenia hippocrepis

The black marking behind the pectoral fin in the shape of a horse-shoe is responsible for the name. It has blue bands around the mouth and an olive green shading to light green on the body and head.

Horse-shoe leatherjacket makes good eating.

HABITAT AND GROWTH
This species is common to all southern States. Generally found off-shore on sand, close to reefs. It grows to a length of 50 cm (20 in).

FISHING
A 1/0 long-shanked hook on a 4 to 5 kg (9 to 11 lb) line is the best rig. Prawns and any fish baits are suitable. Use rig no. 9.

LEATHERJACKET, ROUGH
Scobinichthys granulatus

It is a dull green-brown fish with dark blotchings over the back and sides. The skin is rough to the touch. Unlike other species of leatherjackets there is no indentation or recess for the strong spine on the head.

Like all leatherjackets, it is good eating. The rough leatherjacket is easy to clean and prepare for the table.

HABITAT AND GROWTH
It is found in most States, in rivers and bays around old jetties and wharves. It grows to a length of about 25 cm (10 in).

FISHING
Use a luderick rig with a no. 8 or 10 hook and peeled prawn. Fish the piles of wharves and/or jetties.

LEATHERJACKET, SIX-SPINED
Meuschenia freycineti

A six-spined leatherjacket is light green with light-blue lines and blotches all over. The ventral flap has thin blue and yellow lines. It has a dorsal spine above the eye with four rows of barbs. The skin is rough without scales. The caudal fin is dark green with a crescent-shaped blue area. Dorsal and anal fins are yellow.
The flesh is white and firm and very good eating.

HABITAT AND GROWTH
It is not a common fish but occasionally caught in close offshore reefs off Victoria and South Australia where it attains a length of 45 cm (18 in).

FISHING
Usually caught when fishing for other species using a small 1/0 hook and prawn, squid or most fish bait.

LEATHERJACKET, SPINY-TAILED
Bigener brownii

Another of the 50-odd species of leatherjackets dispersed around our coast. It is green, with blue spots and bright blue lines about the mouth and the usual trigger spike above the eyes.
Again, it is good eating.

HABITAT AND GROWTH
Generally found on near-coastal rocky reefs. A bottom-dweller, it grows to a length of 45 cm (18 in).

FISHING
Use a 5 kg (11 lb) line, a no. 1 long shanked hook and rig no. 9. Any usual fish bait, prawn or squid will suffice.

LEATHERJACKET, YELLOW-FINNED
Meuschenia trachylepis

Generally olive-green with three or four wide dark longitudinal bands, sometimes broken. The fins are a pale yellow except for the blotched tail. There is a single strong serrated spine above the eye.

The flesh is firm and very good eating.

HABITAT AND GROWTH
It is quite common in inshore waters and inlets along the New South Wales and southern Queensland coast where it attains a length of 40 cm (16 in).

FISHING
It has a very small mouth and a long shanked no. 1 hook is best. Use a light 5 kg (11 lb) line; bait can be prawn, squid, octopus, small piece of fish bait and, in fact, most protein baits. Use rig no. 9

PORCUPINE FISH
Dicotylichthys punctulatus

There are several different porcupine fish but this one is the most common. It is generally white with dark spots all over, and is covered in spines. When caught or in danger, it inflates by filling its air bladder causing the spines to stand erect. They are not dangerous to touch. The fish has very sharp teeth.

HABITAT AND GROWTH
Found in all States of Australia and New Zealand in rivers and estuaries. It grows to a length of about 44 cm (17 in).
Caution: The flesh of all porcupine fish is poisonous and *must not be eaten.*

SAW SHARK, COMMON
Pristiophorus cirratus

Body elongated with a long snout and numerous teeth along its edges. Two tentacles hang halfway along the snout.
The flesh is firm, white and good to eat.

HABITAT AND GROWTH
Found in the coastal waters in depths to 300 m (984 ft) in the southern half of Australia, including Tasmania. Grows to about 124 cm (4 ft).

FISHING
Occasionally caught by snapper fishermen. It is not harmful to man.

SHARK, BLUE POINTER
Isurus oxyrhynchus
Also known as Mako

Body is dark blue above to the tip of the pointed snout, and white below, except for the fins, which are greyish. The tailfin is deeply forked.
The flesh of smaller fish is said to be tasty when smoked.

HABITAT AND GROWTH
Found off all Australian States on the Continental Shelf, where it grows to a length of about 4 m (13 ft) and 363 kg (800 lb).

FISHING
Its fighting abilities are legendary. It will readily take a bait or Knucklehead lure, trolled at 8 or 9 knots. The blue pointer shark is dangerous to man.

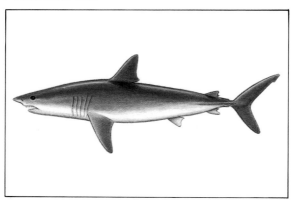

SHARK, BRONZE WHALER
Carcharhinus brachyurus

Closely resembles the common whaler shark, but its back is bronze and its belly is creamy. Its upper teeth have oblique points, and the lower ones are narrow, erect and wide-based. It is also smaller than the whaler. Not highly regarded as a food fish.

HABITAT AND GROWTH
The bronze whaler shark inhabits the open seas off south Queensland and New South Wales. It grows to a length of about 2.7 m (9 ft), and its average weight is about 90 kg (200 lb). It does enter bays and estuaries and can be dangerous to man.

FISHING
Every bit as good a fighter, pound for pound, as a whaler, it is chased by big game fishermen. Usual big game tackle and techniques.

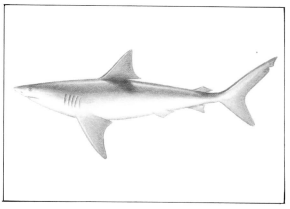

SHARK, GREY NURSE
Odontaspis taurus

A large shark, dangerous to man. It has an array of awl-like teeth. The body is grey above and white below.

HABITAT AND GROWTH
It is found in all Australian States and generally inhabits the open sea where it attains a length of 5 m (16 ft). It feeds on tuna, mackerel, salmon and other pelagic fish.

FISHING
Game fishing gear and tactics, either with a floating fishbait in a berley slick, or trolling. In an unofficial conservation move, most game fishermen leave this shark alone.

SHARK, GUMMY
Mustelus antarcticus

The gummy shark is not dangerous to man, as the name 'shark' might suggest. It is very streamlined, with a long tapered head, grey above the lateral line with a lighter shade below and darker grey fin tips. The teeth are flat and smooth.
  Good eating.

HABITAT AND GROWTH
Ranges on the Continental Shelf from southern Queensland south and along the Victorian, South Australian and southern half of the Western Australian coast. Grows to about 160 cm (5 ft 3 in). The young are born as self-sufficient juveniles. It feeds on shellfish, worms and other invertebrates.

FISHING
The basis of a substantial commercial fishery in the southern States. However, mercury content has been a bone of contention and fishing was suspended for a time. Caught by longline, it is sold as 'flake'.

SHARK, HAMMERHEAD
Sphyrna lewini

This shark is easily identified by its hammer-like head. The eyes are perched on the extremities of its head. The body is dark grey above, creamy below.
  Rarely eaten.

HABITAT AND GROWTH
The hammerhead shark is found generally in the open sea but occasionally in the estuaries where it grows to at least 5 m (16 ft). It is a shark dangerous to man and is found along the coasts of all Australian States.

FISHING
A gamefish, it will take baitfish trolled in a manner similar to that which takes marlin.

SHARK, PORT JACKSON
Heterodontus portusjacksoni

The Port Jackson shark is a harmless species growing to about
1.5 m (5 ft) in shallow reefs close to the coast. It is said to be the
oldest of all sharks, dating back millions of years. The body is
brown with prominent charcoal markings on the snout, below
the eyes and on the body. The egg sack is often found on beaches
attached to kelp that comes ashore after a storm. It's a black
tapered cone about the size of a pear, with long curly tendrils for
anchoring to the kelp. Hatching takes place during the fourth
month.

HABITAT AND GROWTH
The Port Jackson shark is slow moving, and lives on shellfish,
crustaceans, sea urchins and anything that doesn't move too
quickly. Widely distributed around the coast on offshore reefs.

FISHING
Often caught at night when fishing for other species.

SHARK, SCHOOL
Galeorhinus australis

Body colour varies from slaty purple to light bluish-grey on the back and much lighter below.

It is very good eating but it must be cleaned soon after landing, or the flesh tastes of ammonia.

HABITAT AND GROWTH

This shark is found in all Australian States but is most common in Bass Strait and around Tasmania. Also found off Lord Howe Island, New Zealand and the Chatham Islands. It is not dangerous to man, and feeds on other fish. It is a bottom dweller which lives on the Continental Shelf and slope, to about 600 m.

Young develop in the mother's body and are born in estuaries and bays as self-sufficient juveniles. It can grow to a length of 2 m (6 ft) and 77 kg (170 lb). One 136 cm (53½ in) specimen tagged in 1949 was recaptured in 1977. Estimated at 18 years old when tagged, it had put on only 5 cm (2 in).

FISHING

It is called snapper shark in Victoria, where it has been seriously overfished by professionals. A ban on the sale of shark in 1974, because of an excessive mercury content, will help in restocking. Good sport, and often caught off the beaches at night when tailor and salmon are about. Use a 40 lb line, a 10/0 hook and whole fish or fillet as bait. Use rig no. 10 or 11.

SHARK, SPOTTED WOBBEGONG
Orectolobus maculatus

Wobbegong, or carpet sharks as they are often called, have a body patterned with symmetrical designs in shades of brown and grey. The mouth is fringed with fleshy, stringy growths. Not a man-eater but on a number of occasions one has darted from the bottom and bitten the rubber swim flipper of a skindiver, apparently mistaking it for a fish. This shark is protected

HABITAT AND GROWTH
Lives among the rocky weed-covered areas near the southern
coast where it grows to about 3 m (10 ft).
FISHING
Not usually sought.

SHARK, THRESHER
Alopias vulpinus

The thresher shark is identified immediately by the very long tail
that is almost as long as the body. It is blue-green above and
white below. It is harmless to man. Rarely eaten.

HABITAT AND GROWTH
It attains a length of 5 metres (16 ft) and can weigh to 418 kg
(920 lb). It is found from Queensland to Western Australia,
including Tasmania. The long tail is used to concentrate small
fish on which it feeds.

FISHING
A gamefish, it will take a trolled baitfish.

27

SHARK, TIGER
Galeocerdo cuvieri

Body cylindrical with a rather blunt snout, bluish-grey above fading to white below with prominent dark vertical bands on the back and sides. It is these markings which give the species its name. The gill slits are noticeably small. Rarely eaten.

HABITAT AND GROWTH
The shark is large, growing to at least 5 m (16 ft) and is dangerous to man. It is found in coastal waters off all States in Australia.

FISHING
Big game fishing gear and techniques are used. Sometimes takes a trolled bait, but more often the boat will anchor over a reefy bottom and float out a slick of berley and a floating whole fish bait.

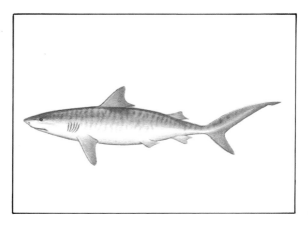

SHARK, WHALER
Carcharhinus obscurus
Also known as Black Whaler or River Shark.

A heavy-bodied shark with a moderately rounded snout and five gill slits. The colour varies from brownish to dark grey above to dull whitish below. The tips of the fins are often blackish or dusky. It is a proven man-eater, and not sought as a food-fish. Its upper teeth are roughly triangular and serrated; its bottom teeth are smaller and narrower. Rarely eaten.

HABITAT AND GROWTH
Whaler shark is basically an open ocean fish, but it can be found in estuaries as far up as the freshwater. It is probably the most commonly found shark in Queensland and New South Wales estuaries. It is the biggest of the whaler sharks in Australian waters, growing to a length of about 3.6 m (12 ft) and weight of about 400 kg (880 lb). It feeds on shoaling mullet, stingrays and even porcupine fish.

FISHING
It is a lively and tenacious fighter when hooked, and many game fishermen prefer it to the tiger shark. It is usually taken by trolling whole baitfish, and using big game tackle.

SHARK, WHITE
Carcharodon carcharias
Also known as White Pointer and White Death.

A streamlined, greyish-white body with white below. It has a fairly straight back and unlike most other sharks, the upper lobe of the tail is not much larger than the lower. It also lacks the pronounced extension of most other species, which gives it great speed through the water. A distinguishing feature is the large triangular and serrated teeth in both jaws.
   Not sought as a food fish.

HABITAT AND GROWTH
The largest dangerous shark in the world, it lives off the southern Australian coast, from southern Queensland round to Western

Australia, but has not been recorded in Tasmanian waters. It grows to a length of about 12 m (40 ft) and a weight of almost 1 tonne. It will eat almost anything, including seals, dolphins, other sharks, and ships' garbage. A roamer of ocean waters, it is rarely seen in estuaries. Nevertheless, it is a known man-eater.

FISHING
Its weight alone makes it a top prize for game fishermen. October to May seem to be the most popular fishing times, but with the demise of the whaling industry, the most prolific white shark feeding areas off the whaling stations have disappeared, and catches are expected to slacken as anglers are forced to hunt the big sharks.

SHARK, ZEBRA

Stegostoma fasciatum
Also known as Leopard Shark.

This is a slender-bodied shark with a long caudal fin. A pronounced bony ridge extends along the back. Juveniles like the one shown here have a series of yellow stripes over a dark brown background. As the shark matures the body and fins become a light brown, and a profusion of dark brown spots develops. It has a small mouth and is harmless to man. Rarely eaten.

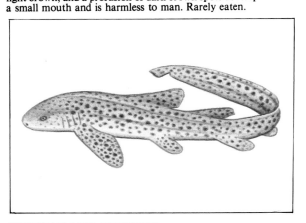

HABITAT AND GROWTH
The zebra shark ranges the coast north from Sydney around to the top half of Western Australia. It feeds on shellfish and grows to about 3 m (10 ft). Very docile, it lays eggs in a black horny case, similar to the Port Jackson shark, which it attaches to kelp.

FISHING
Not usually fished for, but often observed by skin divers.

STINGRAY, BLUE-SPOTTED
Amphotistius kuhlii

The tail, which is short, is armed with a serrated spine that is capable of inflicting a painful wound. It is brownish with broad pale blue spots and smaller black spots on the back creamy-white

underneath. It propels itself by undulating its wide flaps.
Not poisonous to eat.

HABITAT AND GROWTH
There are numerous species of stingrays. The blue-spotted
stingray occurs throughout waters of tropical and subtropical
Australia and grows to about 78 cm (31 in). Often caught by
trawlers.

FISHING
Usually caught when drifting for flathead or when fishing the
beaches. Not sought.

Caution: Care must be exercised in handling, as the serrated barb
on the tail can inflict a painful wound.

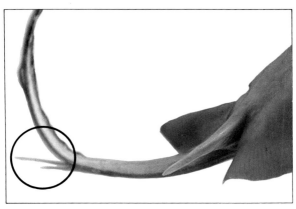

STONEFISH, REEF
Synanceia verucosa

An unattractive fish, its stone-yellow skin is covered with wart-
like growths which help its efforts at camouflage. Its general
shape resembles that of a scorpionfish.

This very ugly fish frequents coral, mud and rocks and could easily be mistaken for a stone. It seldom moves and anything that settles on it is pierced by 13 long sharp spines which release a poison when the covering skin is depressed.

HABITAT AND GROWTH
It is capable of living 24 hours out of the water. Stonefish are prevalent all over the Great Barrier Reef and the Gulf of Carpentaria area, and as far south as Moreton Bay where they have been seen in inlets and bays. Grows to 45 cm (18 in).

FISHING
Avoided, rather than sought.

Caution: The poison can be fatal. A victim should be given mouth-to-mouth resuscitation while being taken to hospital for the antidote. As a temporary measure, acetic acid, urine, vinegar, a preparation called Stingose or methylated spirits can be applied to the punctures.

TRIGGERFISH, BROWN
Sufflamen fraenatus
Also called the Bridled Triggerfish.

A drab brownish fish with a pale streak running from the mouth along the chin. This triggerfish is a notorious bait-stealer and its tough armoured skin makes it unpopular with fishermen.

HABITAT AND GROWTH
This is a tropical fish and ranges the entire top half of Australia above the Tropic of Capricorn. It occurs around reefs and attains a length of 30 cm (12 inches).

FISHING
It is sometimes caught when fishing for other species but seldom specially sought after.

TRIGGERFISH, STARRY
Abalistes stellatus

Also known as Flat-tailed Triggerfish.

Generally pale olive-green, the starry triggerfish has three distinct white blotches high on the back near the fins. The upper body carries numerous blue spots and underneath around the belly larger yellow blotches, all of which can fade shortly after capture. The dorsal and anal fins have blue and yellow bands, the caudal is brown-spotted.

Though flesh is white and firm and good tasting, this fish is not edible because it is thought to be poisonous.

HABITAT AND GROWTH
This fish ranges the entire Queensland coast, and the top half of Western Australia where it grows to 61 cm (24 in). It is a coral reef species.

FISHING
The starry triggerfish has always been suspect for ciguatera poisoning and therefore considered unacceptable as a table fish.

CHAPTER TWO

Flat Fish

FLATHEAD, ARMOURED
Hoplichthys haswelli
Also known as Deep-sea Flathead.

There is no mistaking this fish as anything but a flathead, but it is unusual because of the heavy bony armour covering it. It is a uniform reddish-brown over the back.

It is a presentable table fish.

HABITAT AND GROWTH
It ranges from Sydney down along the bottom half of Australia, including Tasmania, and the southern portion of Western Australia. It grows to 43 cm (17 in).

FISHING
This is a trawl fish but is occasionally caught on a handline while fishing for other species.

FLATHEAD, DUSKY
Platycephalus fuscus

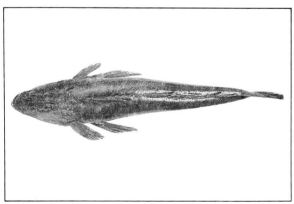

Its upper surface is almost black, and underneath is white. It has small fine teeth which are exceedingly sharp in a large mouth.

Body is elongated and depressed.
Flesh is dry, firm and white; good eating.

HABITAT AND GROWTH
This species of flathead is found in tidal rivers, lakes, bays and estuaries and on shallow flats just offshore. It is the largest flathead, and has been known to grow to length of 1.5 m (60 in) and weigh over 10 kg (22 lb). Found in all Australian States. Most are taken during January to March when the fish move down the river to spawn. They bury themselves in sand or mud with their eyes clear and prey on small fish and crustaceans.

FISHING
As with all flathead, a moving bait is best and any fish fillet is effective, although live yellowtail and poddy mullet are recommended. Use a 7 kg (15 lb) line, a 4/0 hook and a short wire trace and rig no. 14 or 15.

It will take a slow-moving artificial lure such as a wobbler — rig no. 6 or 8. Fishing from the shore, use the same rig but live bait is more effective than strip bait. Small yellowtail, mullet or tailor about 13 cm (5 in) long are ideal, but make sure you push the hook through the back about half way between head and tail, avoiding the backbone. Cast into the channel or the deep water along the bank. Use a wire trace and allow the flathead time to swallow the bait and the hook. When he first bites he has only the bait in his mouth, so don't put any weight on the line until he turns and starts to swim away. Then strike hard. Don't try to lift him out of the water by the line; use a net or gaff or swim him to a convenient shallow spot. An ebb tide is always best for flathead.

FLATHEAD, ROCK
Leviprora laevigata

It has brown spots on the back and sides and is white underneath. The mouth is large with small teeth. All fins other than anal are covered with brown spots.
The firm white flesh is good eating.

HABITAT AND GROWTH
This species seems to prefer the colder waters of the south-west Western Australian coast, South Australia, Victoria, Tasmania and the southern New South Wales coast. It is bottom-dwelling in reef areas with scattered mud and sand, where it grows to a length of 50 cm (20 in.)

FISHING
Rock flathead will take most fish baits and can be caught on an Arundel Wobbler or similar lure trolled very slowly. Use 7 kg (15 lb) line, a 4/0 hook and rig no. 11.

FLATHEAD, SAND
Platycephalus arenarius

The sand flathead has three or four dark bands on the upper half and two black bars on the lower half. It is a light to mid-brown with creamy spots all over the upper half and creamy lower half.
   The dry white flesh of the sand flathead is good eating.

HABITAT AND GROWTH
This species is found on coastal beaches and grows to a length of 46 cm (18 in). It travels in schools and feeds on small baitfish, prawns and squid by lying half-buried in sand at the edge of a channel or gutter.

FISHING
Fish the deep edge of a gutter on an ocean beach or channel in an estuary. Use 7 kg (15 lb) line and a 4/0 hook and any fish bait. Rig no. 14 or 15 is suitable, but use rig no. 6 or 18 if fishing with a lure. A wobbler is suitable.

FLATHEAD, TIGER
Neoplatycephalus richardsoni

The upper half of the body is dark brown with a series of tiger stripes. The lower half is creamy-white.
   Tiger flathead is good eating.

HABITAT AND GROWTH
It lives in the sandy patches near or among rocky coastal outcrops and in a similar environment in estuaries. Tiger flathead ranges along the entire coastline of New South Wales and Victoria but is particularly plentiful around Cape Everard and Mallacoota. It grows to a length of 64 cm (25 in) and a weight of about 1.3 kg (3 lb).

FISHING
Flathead will take most fish baits but prefers them on the move. Use a 5-7 kg (12-15 lb) nylon line with a 3/0 hook, a light wire

trace and rig no. 11. Can be caught with a very slow-moving artificial lure similar to the Arundel Wobbler.

FLOUNDER, GREENBACK
Rhombosolea tapirina
Also known as Melbourne flounder.

The upper surface of the body is greenish, greyish or brownish, with or without dark blotches. Lower surface is white. An excellent eating fish, the flesh is moist and succulent.

HABITAT AND GROWTH
This species is the largest and most abundant flounder in southern Australian waters. It generally lives on sandy or muddy bottoms in deep bays and estuaries. Attains a length of 40 cm (16 in).

FISHING
It will take most baits. Use a 1/0 hook on a 5 kg (11 lb) line and rig no. 9.

FLOUNDER, LARGE-TOOTHED
Pseudorhombus arsius

This species is light brown on top with blotches all over. Sometimes the blotches disappear, and the flounder is capable of changing colour to suit the environment. Its name derives from its exceptionally large teeth. This is a good fish for eating.

HABITAT AND GROWTH
Large-toothed flounder can be found all around Australia and although generally caught on sand near the estuary mouth, it can sometimes be caught in depths of up to 55 m (30 fathoms) further seaward. It grows to a length of 38 cm (15 in).

FISHING
It will take most baits, but prawns are best. Use a 1/0 hook on a 5 kg (11 lb) line and rig no. 9.

FLOUNDER, LONG-SNOUTED
Ammotretis rostratus

Light brown on top — which can change slightly to suit the

environment — and white underneath. It is a flat fish and both eyes are on top and close together.

Like all flounder, the long-snouted variety is superb eating. The flesh is firm and white, with delicate texture and flavour.

HABITAT AND GROWTH
It occurs in southern Queensland, along the New South Wales coast, Victoria, Western Australia and Tasmania. It lives in sandy weed patches in coastal bays and close offshore sand patches. It grows to a length of 30 cm (12 in).

FISHING
It is caught on the bottom, using worms, prawns or nippers for bait. Use a 3 kg (6 lb) line on a slow drift with a running sinker, a 1 m trace and a no. 6 hook. Use rig no. 4, 9 or 16.

FLOUNDER
SMALL-TOOTHED
Pseudorhombus jenynsii

Light brown with an overall pattern on the upper half and white underneath. It is a flatfish with both eyes on top and close together.

The flesh is white and very good eating.

HABITAT AND GROWTH
Small-toothed flounder are found in all Australian States, in Bass Strait and around Tasmania. It attains a length of 34 cm (14 in). It lives on sand and mud in all depths on the Continental Shelf.

FISHING
Use a 1/0 hook with a 5 kg (10 or 12 lb) line and rig no. 4. Prawn is the best bait.

RAY, BANKS' SHOVELNOSE

Aptychotrema rostrata
Often referred to as a Shovelnose Shark because of its tail, which resembles that of a shark.

Colouring resembles that of a sand flathead — sandy brown on

top with creamy-white underneath. It swims by undulating its huge flaps. It has no venomous spines to trouble you.

The flesh is white and tastes good; it is sold as 'flake'.

HABITAT AND GROWTH
This is the common species often caught off the southern half of Queensland, all along the New South Wales coast and along the southern shore of Australia and the southern half of Western Australia. It frequents sandy beaches and areas of sand and mud. It grows to a length of about 122 cm (48 in).

FISHING
Usually caught when fishing for flathead.

SOLE, BLACK
Achylopa nigra

Olive-brown to dark brown, with numerous darker blotches all over the upper surfaces of the body, head and fins. Creamy underneath with both eyes on the upper side.

The flesh is firm and white and very good eating.

HABITAT AND GROWTH
It prefers sandy areas with ribbon weed in bays and ports around Australia. Grows to about 41 cm (16 in). The average fish caught is about 33 cm (13 in).

FISHING
Fish the bottom on a slow drift and use prawn, yabbie, or worm on a no. 1 hook, a light 3 kg (6 lb) line and rig no. 4.

SOLE, LEMON TONGUE
Paraplagusia unicolor

This species of sole is not oval-shaped like the others, but elongated. It is olive-brown to dark brown and white underneath. The eyes are on top and close together.
Lemon tongue sole makes good eating.

HABITAT AND GROWTH
It prefers sand and sand/mud patches in the bays and estuaries in the southern half of the continent. Grows to about 38 cm (15 in).

FISHING
Use prawn, yabbie or worm on a slow drift over sand and mud patches. Use a no. 6 hook on a light 3 kg (6 lb) line and rig no. 4.

SOLE, NARROW-BANDED
Aseraggodes macleayanus

Olive-brown with a number of dark narrow bands running the

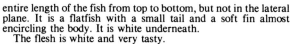

entire length of the fish from top to bottom, but not in the lateral plane. It is a flatfish with a small tail and a soft fin almost encircling the body. It is white underneath.

The flesh is white and very tasty.

HABITAT AND GROWTH
Prefers sandy areas or areas of sand silt in the southern half of the continent in harbours and bays in coastal waters. It grows to a length of about 33 cm (13 in). The average fish caught is about 26 cm (10 in). Narrow-banded sole is particularly plentiful around Mooloolabah, Queensland. It conceals itself by partly burying in the sand.

FISHING
Narrow-banded sole is a bottom dweller which prefers worms, green prawns or yabbies on a slow drift over sand or mud. Use a no. 1 hook, a light 3 kg (6 lb) line and rig no. 4.

SOLE, PEACOCK
Achirus pavoninus

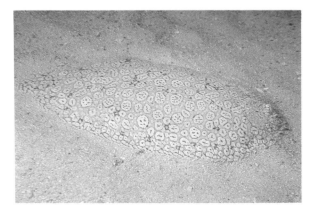

Brown with green splotches all over the body and fins.
The flesh is good eating.

HABITAT AND GROWTH
It prefers the warm waters of Queensland and frequents bays and
estuaries on the mainland where there is sand and mud. Grows
only to about 25 cm (10 in).

FISHING
Not usually fished for because of its small size.

CHAPTER THREE

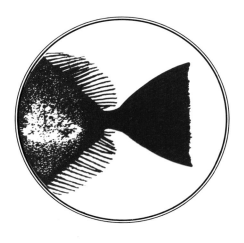

Fish with a Straight Tail Fin

BATFISH, HUMPHEADED
Platax batavianus

Slate brown on the upper body and silvery below. As it ages the fish develops humps on the snout in the same way as snapper. A wide vertical bar running across the eye and head is a characteristic marking.

It is a thick, robust fish and a strong swimmer, but poor eating.

HABITAT AND GROWTH
Fairly common in warmer climates and found around reefs when fishing for other species, such as sweetlip and coral trout. It grows quite large, around 4.5 kg (10 lb) and up to 56 cm (22 in) long.

FISHING
Batfish is rarely fished for, and is caught on northern coral reefs when angling for other reef species.

COD, PURPLE

Epinephelus hoedti
Also known as Blue Maori.

To southerners it resembles a wirrah in body shape and colour. It is a thick-bodied fish, predominantly greenish-brown, tending to purple with numerous dark spots covering the entire head, body and fins.

Unlike the wirrah, the flesh of the purple rock cod is white and firm, and rates high in table quality.

HABITAT AND GROWTH
A tropical fish found as far south as northern New South Wales, but generally above the Capricorn line from Queensland to Western Australia. Purple rock cod frequents the coral reefs where it is known to grow to a length of 100 cm (40 in) although fish this size are rarely taken by anglers.

FISHING
It is not specially fished for, but rather caught when fishing for other reef fish. A strong fighter, it will put up a creditable performance to stay in its coral home on the bottom. Although it grows much larger, the usual run of fish taken is about 45 to 50 cm long (17 to 20 in). To land a fish of that size among the coral you need a line of 22 kg (50 lb) breaking strain and a strong 6/0 hook. Any fish bait will do and use rig no. 9 or 16.

COD, RED ROCK
Scorpaena cardinalis
Also known as Red Scorpion Cod, Fire Cod, and Prickly Heat.

This has a rather gruesome-looking head covered with spines, a large mouth and is bright red with creamy blotches. Handle with caution, because the sharp spines on and around the head are capable of inflicting painful stab wounds; however, they are not dangerous.

The flesh is snow white, tender and of excellent flavour.

HABITAT AND GROWTH
This species grows to about 46 cm (18 in) but the average is 22-25 cm (9-10 in). Red rock cod lives in kelp beds and on the shallow reefs offshore and is rarely taken in deep water. Found along the coasts of Tasmania, New South Wales and Queensland.

FISHING
Usually caught when fishing for snapper and morwong. It lives on crab and small fish. When preparing the fish for the table, it is

best to cut the head right away, fillet and skin.

Caution: Handle with care. Avoid contact with the spines around the head and the fins. The sting is not serious but it is unpleasant.

COD, SADDLED
Epinephelus daemelii

The young fish are mottled grey with six vivid vertical bands of darker tones. When fully grown they are dark grey, the bands having faded out except for a patch on the upper surface of the butt of the tail. It's a bulky, thick-bodied fish with a large mouth.

The smaller individuals weighing about 4 kg (9 lb) are excellent table fish.

HABITAT AND GROWTH
This species can grow to around 45 kg (100 lb) but a fish that size is coarse and not good eating. Found on the east coast of Australia as far south as Sydney, in northern Australia, Papua New Guinea and Lord Howe Island. It frequents offshore reefs both close and wide and on occasions is caught in the estuaries.

FISHING
For the smaller fish, use a 7 kg (15 lb) line and a 4/0 hook and cunjevoi or fish bait. Use rig no. 9 or 16.

DORY, JOHN
Zeus faber

John dory is dark brown with a large round spot on both sides of its body, about the middle. The spots are said to be the imprints of the Lord's thumb and forefinger. It is a short, deep-bodied fish with a large mouth that can extend considerably.

A much sought-after table fish that brings high prices at the market.

HABITAT AND GROWTH
Frequents offshore reefs and at certain times, estuaries and harbours around New South Wales, Tasmania, Western Australia and as far north as Bundaberg, Queensland. Has been known to grow to 60 cm (24 in) but the average is about 500 g (1 lb).

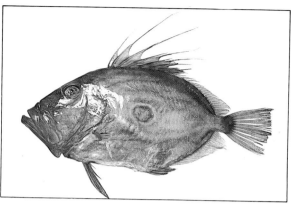

FISHING

Trawled for extensively but will usually take live fish as bait, or at best, very fresh fillets. Use a 3/0 hook, about 7 kg (15 lb) line and rig no. 15.

DORY, MIRROR

Zenopsis nebulosus

Mirror dory has the same dark blotch as its relative, the John dory. It is a short deep-bodied fish with a large mouth that can extend considerably. The body is silver, smooth and free of scales. The ventral fins are very long, as is the first portion of the dorsal fin. It resembles John dory with a turned-up snout.

Very good eating.

HABITAT AND GROWTH

It is found in waters of New South Wales, Victoria, South Australia, north-west Australia and Tasmania in depths to 130 m where it grows to 46 cm (18 in).

FISHING

Rarely caught on a line, it is mostly taken by trawlermen. It will take a bait but most dory prefer live food, ignoring strips of flesh. The preferred rig for mirror dory is no. 15 using a 6/0 hook.

49

DORY, SILVER
Cyttus australis

Similar to the John dory in shape and size, but a silvery colour without the characteristic thumb marks.

The flesh is white and it is a good table fish.

HABITAT AND GROWTH
Little is known about the species, except that it ranges in colder waters south of latitude 33°. Large hauls have been made off New South Wales, Victoria, South Australia, the southern half of Western Australia and Tasmania.

FISHING
Caught almost exclusively by professionals fishing beyond the Continental Shelf; usually netted.

GALAXIAS, COMMON
Galaxias maculatus
Also known as Native Trout.

In New South Wales it is known as jollytail, and in Victoria and South Australia is sometimes referred to as pulangi. The native trout is often thought to be a young rainbow, but it lacks scales and the dorsal fin. Yellow, with blotches of mauve and speckled with black.

HABITAT AND GROWTH
This native species is found in coastal streams of Tasmania, Victoria, South Australia, southern Queensland and New South Wales. Eggs are carried to sea on vegetation where they hatch, the young fry returning upstream to fresh water where they mature. They grow to only 15 cm (6 in).

FISHING
Fished for only as baitfish. Use a light rod and reel, a 3 kg (6 lb) line with shrimp, earthworms, crickets, grasshoppers, beetles and woodgrubs. Use rig no. 20, 21 or 22. Check local trout fishing laws before wetting a line.

GROPER, EASTERN BLUE
Achoerodus viridis

The body is deep and robust, generally bluish in maturity and greenish in juveniles. Some reddish-brown specimens are often called red or brown groper, but scientists now believe they are the same species. In the front of the upper and lower jaws the groper has heavy lips and four large teeth, which it uses to crunch crustaceans, shellfish, cunjevoi, sea urchin and starfish.

The flesh of the groper is white, flaky, a little fatty, and considered one of our best table fish.

HABITAT AND GROWTH
The eastern blue groper inhabits rocky coastlines of New South Wales and Victoria. A related species, the western blue groper *(Achoerodus gouldii)* occurs in South Australia and the more temperate waters of Western Australia. A 12 kg (26 lb) fish is considered large, although fish to 50 kg (110 lb) have been recorded. Not a travelling fish, it prefers to live in family groups in the same area, a habit which makes it vulnerable to spear-fishermen. By 1969 stocks had been so depleted in New South Wales, a total ban was placed on taking this prized fish by any method. The ban still applies to spearfishing, but you may now take it by a line. Its favourite food is the red crab found in red weedbeds on rocky shores.

FISHING

A very stout rod and line must be used because as soon as the groper is hooked it darts headlong into a crevice or cave, and all the pulling in the world won't budge it. The hook has to be heavy duty and the line strong enough to pull the fish to you. Use 23 kg (50 lb) line, a heavy duty 4/0 hook and rig no. 17. Red crab is the best bait.

GURNARD, RED

Chelidonichthys kumu

Predominantly red with silvery-white undersides, the fins fan out and are spectacularly coloured with blue spots. The head is large and bony but without the characteristic sharp projection of the flying gurnard, with which it is often confused.

The flesh is good eating.

HABITAT AND GROWTH

The red gurnard inhabits the entire Australian coast as well as New Zealand and South African waters. It grows to a length of 62 cm (24 in) but most fish captured are about 41 cm (16 in).

FISHING

Red gurnard is not particularly sought but is often caught on sandy patches on or near offshore reefs when fishing for other species.

HORSEHEAD, WARD'S

Branchiostegus wardi

Also known as a Tile Fish.

This fish has a reddish body with mauve tonings, golden yellow fins and a snout the shape of a horsehead by which it derives its name. The caudal fin is straight and has a dark blotch on the lower half.

It is a white fleshed fish and the texture is fine. It is not rated highly as a table fish.

HABITAT AND GROWTH

A ward's horsehead is found in deep water on sand, mud, and gravel bottom from Port Stephens, New South Wales, north to Noosa, Queensland. It attains a length of 45 cm (17 in).

FISHING

A fish caught when fishing for other species such as snapper and flathead.

JAVELIN, SPOTTED

Pomadasys nageb

The spotted javelin has an overall silvery look with a golden tint on the underside of the body. Mature fish develop a mauve tint above the lateral line with numerous brown spots. Often referred to as grunter as they make a rather loud grunting noise when boated.

The flesh is firm and white and good eating.

HABITAT AND GROWTH

Plentiful in north Queensland and the northern Australian waters where it inhabits the mangrove-lined tidal creeks and bays. It grows to 7 kg (15 lb) and 60 cm (24 in) but fish of 1-2 kg (2-4 lb) are most likely to be caught.

FISHING

Use a small live baitfish such as hardyhead or small mullet, and a 4/0 hook, a 7 kg (15 lb) nylon line and rig no. 4 or 15. They will also take prawn and a fresh fillet of baitfish.

53

LONG-TOM, FRESHWATER
Strongylura kreffti

There are about 12 different species of long-tom in Australian waters, some growing to almost 2 m (6 ft). Generally similar to a garfish in shape with two long beaks and very sharp teeth. Singly, or in schools, they can leap from the water and 'fly' over the surface with only the tail submerged for a number of metres.

Delicious to eat, but their green bones cause some people to have doubts about them.

HABITAT AND GROWTH
This is the only long-tom which occurs in freshwater in Australia and is distributed in larger streams throughout the tropical north. Feeds on smaller fishes.

FISHING
Best caught with a small strip of fish bait on a 1/0 hook using a 5 kg (11 lb) nylon line and rig no. 23.

PARROT-FISH, SURF
Scarus rivulatus

Brilliantly coloured, the pattern changes with growth. Recognisable by the blue-edged, red colouring of the anal fin. The middle of the dorsal fin is spotted green and the tips are brilliant blue.

The flesh is firm and white and very good eating, although not particularly sought.

HABITAT AND GROWTH
The surf parrot-fish is abundant in the tropics and ranges from the coral cays and reefs of the Great Barrier Reef to similar terrain in Western Australia. As the tide rises it enters the coral fringed lagoons and can often be seen feeding in shallow pools where it is caught on a falling tide. It is adept at camouflage and will often hide undetected in a coral crevice. This species grows to a weight of about 3 kg (6 lb).

FISHING
Not especially fished for with lines, but occasionally caught when fishing for other species. More easily caught by hand in shallow coral pools as the tide recedes.

PIGFISH, FRENCH'S
Bodianus frenchii

There are several species of pigfish, but this one is orange-pink with rather large scales, moderate-sized mouth and broad lips.

It has two prominent yellowish spots on the back.

The flesh is firm and white and it is a good table fish.

HABITAT AND GROWTH
The pigfish is a reef dweller, most often found on deeper reefs around the coast of the southern half of Australia. It grows to a length of 45 cm (18 in).

FISHING
Rarely fished for, but caught when fishing for snapper on the wider reefs. Because snapper fishermen usually prefer a 4/0 or 5/0 hook, and the mouth of the pigfish is too small for such a hook, only a few are ever taken. If the correct size hook was used, say a 2/0, many good snapper would be lost. Snapper rig no. 16. It will take any fresh fish bait, prawn, squid, and octopus.

55

WRASSE, CRIMSON BANDED
Pseudolabrus gymnogenis

♂

The most distinguishing marking is a crimson band around the body through the front of the dorsal fin and the rear part of the anal fin. When young, the fish has numerous white spots but as it grows, the spots disappear. The colouring is then generally brown and bright red fins with tones of orange and yellow. A bulky, blunt body.

The flesh is firm, but off-white, and not good eating.

HABITAT AND GROWTH
Its habitat is the rocky coast and shallow reefs close to the shore. It is found in southern Queensland and New South Wales. It grows only to a length of 31 cm (12 in).

FISHING
Caught while fishing for other species. The fish has a small mouth and a 1/0 hook on a 4 kg (9 lb) nylon line will suffice. Most fish baits, prawns, crab and cunjevoi are effective. Use rig no. 13.

WRASSE, MAORI
Opthalmolepis lineolatus
Sometimes called the Rainbow Fish.

This beautifully coloured fish is red on top with a white band along the lateral line, a blue band below it and creamy underneath. Numerous blue and purple Maori markings surround the head and eyes. It has scales but its blunt body is slimy and difficult to hold.

Its white flesh is among the best of the wrasse family.

HABITAT AND GROWTH
Rainbow fish are very common close to the NSW coast on reefs and are also found around the southern mainland coast. It can grow to about 50 cm (20 in) but is usually around 33 cm (13 in). Lives in similar habitat to Groper.

FISHING
Caught when fishing for other species. It has a small mouth and

a no. 2 hook is large enough. Any prawn or fish will do. It is a bottom-feeding fish. Use a 4 kg (9 lb) nylon line and rig no. 9.

WRASSE, VIOLET-LINED MAORI
Cheilinus digrammus

Green over the head, back and tail and the belly is a light red, which extends to the central and anal fins. The tail is rounded and yellow-edged. A series of Maori markings of light red on the head near the eyes identifies this fish.

The flesh is firm and good eating.

HABITAT AND GROWTH
It is common in the tropical north, where it inhabits the coral reefs and grows to about 38 cm (15 in).

FISHING
Caught when fishing for other reef species. It will readily take any fishbait, prawn or crab.

CHAPTER FOUR

Fish with a Convex Tail Fin

BARRAMUNDI
Lates calcarifer
Also known as Giant Perch, and Palmer Perch.

Dark bluish-grey on the upper body and silver below, with a yellow tinge on the caudal fin. The eyes are a bright pinkish-red and glow at night. It is a deep-bodied fish with a large mouth and powerful tail. The word 'barramundi' was used by Aborigines for three river fish with large scales — *Scleropages leichhardti* (saratoga) and *Neoceratodus forsteri* (Queensland lungfish). Today the name is almost universally applied to *Lates calcarifer*.
Its flesh is white, tender and firm, and extremely tasty.

HABITAT AND GROWTH
The fish probably rates as Australia's number one recreational fish. Caught in both fresh and salt water, it is great sport and delicious on the table. It has been known to grow upwards of 45 kg (100 lb) but heavy fishing has greatly reduced numbers. The average fish caught now seldom exceeds 3 kg (6 lb). It is widely distributed in coastal rivers and estuaries in the tropical and semi-tropical Indo-Pacific regions from Japan to the Persian Gulf. In Australia, barramundi range from the Mary River in Queensland, around the northern coast to Roebourne in Western Australia.
It spawns in estuaries or brackish coastal waters in the wet season from about October to March. Juveniles move upstream during each flood, while newly-matured adults move down. It seems to be plentiful in river systems with large catchment areas, muddy or sandy beds, a sluggish, meandering flow and slow discharge. It's an hermaphrodite, changing from male to female at roughly two years of age.

FISHING
Fish on a rising tide at dusk in tidal waters for best results, using small whole live fish, large prawn or live frog on a 6/0 hook and a 15 kg (34 lb) nylon line and rig no. 6 or 15. Many are caught with lures: the A.B.U. Killer type is most popular.

BEARDIE
Lotella rhacinus

Has some resemblance to a ling fish but more robust, and is often mistaken for a bearded rock cod. Of the two dorsal fins, the first

has only six or seven spines, the second extends to the tail. The fins are brown; the tail fin is rounded. It has a single barbel under the mouth.

It is a reddish-brown above and creamy below; and good eating.

HABITAT AND GROWTH
Beardie are found on offshore reefs to 90 metres in the southern half of the continent including Tasmania, where they grow to 50 cm (20 in). Fish about 35 cm (14 in) are more common.

FISHING
Often caught when fishing for snapper and other reef-dwelling species. They will take most fresh fish bait, prawns and hermit crab. Use a 3/0 hook on a 9 kg (20 lb) line and rig no. 16.

BLACKFISH, RIVER
Gadopsis marmoratus

Body elongate and rounded. Brown on top with dark streaks and blotches and golden below. A single long dorsal fin which projects further from the body as it nears the tail. The anal fin is long and also wider towards the tail. The anal fin and tailfin are rounded.

The flesh is very oily and not good eating.

HABITAT AND GROWTH
This fish likes the cold mountain streams and plenty of shade. It grows to about 60 cm (24 in) and is found in Tasmania, South Australia, Victoria, New South Wales and Queensland. Once it was very common but stocks are becoming depleted. Spawning occurs in spring.

FISHING
Use a no. 6 to no. 1 hook, a float and 1 m (3 ft) leader with yabbies, earthworms, shrimps and wood grubs for bait. A 22 kg (5 lb) line will suffice. Use rig no. 2 or 21.

BULLFISH, FEATHER FIN

Heniochus acuminatus

Also known as Pennant Coralfish.

This fish derives its name from the long filament from the fourth spine of the dorsal fin. This filament is white and this colour continues to the under-belly, either side is a dark band of approximately the same width. The dorsal and caudal fins are bright yellow. The mouth is small.

Feather fin bullfish can be eaten.

HABITAT AND GROWTH
This little fish ranges the entire coast of Queensland and the tropical north of Western Australia and the Torres Straits where it grows to 25 cm (10 in).

FISHING
Feather fin bullfish is a small fish found where fish are generally plentiful and therefore not especially sought after. To have the chance of hooking one you would need to use a no. 8 blackfish hook.

COD, BEARDED ROCK

Pseudophycis barbatus

The bearded rock cod is often confused with the beardie, which it closely resembles. The shape and colouring are similar — reddish brown, but the fins are black-tipped, whereas the fins of the beardie are not. Each has a single barbel under the mouth.

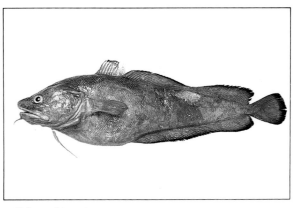

It is good to eat.

HABITAT AND GROWTH
Bearded rock cod is found in southern Australian waters on reefs close offshore and near the ocean front where it grows to about 46 cm (18 in). Fish 35 cm (14 in) are common.

FISHING
Often caught when fishing for other reef-dwelling species, and will readily take any crustacean or fresh fish bait. Use a 2/0 or 3/0 hook on a 9 kg (20 lb) line and rig no. 16.

COD, BLACK-TIPPED ROCK

Epinephelus fasciatus
Also known as Black-tipped Groper and Footballer Cod.

This fish is bright red with a number of bright pink vertical bands, which fade with age. The tips of the dorsal fin are black. The tailfin is rounded and the eye is encircled by a black ring.
  The flesh is firm and white and is prized for the table.

HABITAT AND GROWTH
Black-tipped rock cod is found all along the Queensland coast,

along the north of Australia and the top half of Western Australia. It is a coral reef dweller and attains a weight of about 2 kg (4½ lb). The average fish caught weighs about 1 kg (2 lb).

FISHING
It is quite a common fish and is caught when reef fishing with a handline. Will take most fish baits or crustaceans. Use a 13 kg (30 lb) line, a 4/0 hook and rig no. 16.

COD, BROWN SPOTTED
Promicrops lanceolatus
Also known as Giant Groper

This giant fish is similar to an estuary cod and colour changes with age. Juvenile fish are golden yellow with broad dark bands. It is spotted all over the body and fins and has a large mouth.

Small fish are good eating but the flesh of large fish is coarse and not considered table quality.

HABITAT AND GROWTH
This is the largest fish known in Australian waters. While known to attain a length of 3.6 m (12 ft) and weigh 545 kg (1,200 lb) in other parts of the world the largest specimen reported here weighed 228 kg (634 lb). They do not move about a lot and take up residence in caves. They are bold and will take a good hard look at any intruder, giving divers a scare, but are not dangerous to man.

FISHING
You will need a large bait for this fish and a doggie mackeral or herring on a series of six 16/0 ganged hooks on a wire trace is ideal. A very heavy line is required. Use a 46 kg (100 lb) line and rig no. 10 and if you can land the fish it should be good eating size. Don't kill a large fish unnecessarily.

COD, CORAL
Cephalopholis miniatus

A beautifully coloured fish predominantly red with numerous black-edged blue spots all over the head, body and fins. It is often confused with coral trout, but the rounded caudal fin of the cod is the distinguishing difference.

This is a prized table fish as the flesh is white, firm and flaky.

HABITAT AND GROWTH
Coral cod is found in tropical waters, although occasionally when the waters are warm it is caught a little further south. It inhabits the coral reefs and feeds on the bottom like coral trout. Grows to a length of 46 cm (18 in), but the average fish caught is about 40 cm (16 in).

FISHING
Not a fussy eater and will readily take most fish baits, prawns and other shellfish. Use a 13 kg (30 lb) line, a 4/0 to 5/0 hook and rig no. 9 or 16.

COD, ESTUARY
Epinephelus malabaricus
Also referred to as Greasy Cod, Spotted River Cod, or Estuary Rock Cod.

The estuary cod is olive-green with a number of brown spots randomly scattered. Younger fish have a number of wide, broken vertical bands of a darker shade across their bodies, but in maturity they seem to become a uniform darker colour. Young fish have numerous brown spots. The tail fin is rounded.

Big fish are coarse-textured, but small fish are good eating.

HABITAT AND GROWTH
Estuary cod is one of the largest and most common cod found in tropical estuaries and on coastal reefs. It can reach a length of over 2 m (6 ft).

FISHING
Crayfish and crab are the favourite food of estuary cod. It will depend on how ambitious you are as to the size line and hook you use. But please don't kill a big fish unless you have a good reason to do so.

COD, FLOWERY
Epinephelus fuscoguttatus
Sometimes referred to as a Carpet Cod.

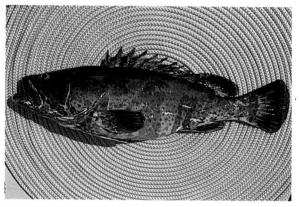

The flowery cod is generally light brown with numerous dark spots and with lighter splotches scattered all over the head, body and fins. All the fins are rounded on the trailing edge and carry a golden green tint on the tips.
The flesh is white and firm, and excellent eating.

HABITAT AND GROWTH
A tropical species which grows to 91 cm (36 in). Flowery cod is caught on coral reefs and in mangrove-lined estuary creeks close to the sea where there is a strong tidal influence.

FISHING
It is usually taken by line fishermen using a 13-22 kg (30-50 lb) line, and 8/0 extra strong hook and a small baitfish or hermit crab. However, it is not a fussy eater and will take most baits. Use rig no. 16.

COD, HONEYCOMB
Epinephelus quoyanus
Also known as Wire Netting Cod and Honeycomb Rock Cod.

It is predominantly brown, with a number of light lines that resemble the pattern of wire netting over the entire fish, including the head and fins.

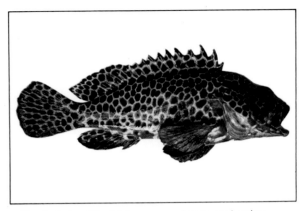

The flesh is white, fairly coarse and very good eating.

HABITAT AND GROWTH
Found all along the Queensland coast where there are reef and rocky outcrops. Honeycomb cod attains a length of about 46 cm (18 in) but most fish caught are about 33 cm (13 in) and weigh about 1 kg (2 lb).

FISHING
Usually caught when fishing for other reef fish such as coral trout and sweetlip. Take care when handling, as the spines of the fins can inflict a painful, although not serious wound. It will readily take most fish baits, prawns, hermit crab. Use rig no. 9 or 16 with a 4/0 to 6/0 strong hook and a 13 kg (30 lb) breaking strain line.

COD, MAORI
Epinephelus undulatostriatus
Also known as Red Speckled Cod.

Body elongate and compressed. A series of fine teeth. The caudal fin is rounded. It is a light brown shade all over with narrow golden stripes. The pectoral fin is bright yellow and all the fins are edged with yellow.
The flesh is firm and white and very good eating.

HABITAT AND GROWTH
It is found on the offshore reefs of northern New South Wales and southern Queensland and around the Swain Reefs. It attains a weight of 5 kg (11 lb).

FISHING
It is usually caught when bottom fishing for snapper and emperor. It is never especially fished for.

COD, MURRAY
Maccullochella peeli

This cod is easily Australia's best-known and most sought freshwater fish. It grows to around 45 kg (100 lb) but heavy fishing is yearly reducing the average weight of fish caught. However, thanks to the foresight of the Inland Fisheries Research Station at Narrandera, New South Wales, rivers are being restocked with fingerlings. Not a fighting fish — in fact lazy.

The table qualities are excellent and at market the fish brings a high price.

HABITAT AND GROWTH
Murray cod is found in the Murray and Darling River systems throughout Victoria, Central Queensland, New South Wales and the headwaters of the Clarence and Richmond Rivers of New South Wales, and the Mary and Dawson Rivers of Queensland.

FISHING
It will take a lure, but most are caught on set lines baited with freshwater yabbies, witchetty grubs and small fish. Use a heavy 13 kg (30 lb) line and 6/0 hooks, and rig no. 4, 15 or 7.

COD, SPECKLE-FINNED
Epinephelus ongus

This is a heavy bodied fish with olive tonings and what appear to be dark spots covering the body, caudal, dorsal and anal fins. The tips of the fins are dark.

The flesh is white and flaky and very good eating.

HABITAT AND GROWTH
It is fairly common in the tropical north of Australia ranging from Bundaberg Queensland, to the same latitude in Western Australia where it inhabits coral reefs and rocky shores. It will enter an estuary on occasions. It grows to about 76 cm (30 in).

FISHING
This fish is caught when reef fishing. It is a strong fighter and a good heavy line is required to keep it from darting into the coral. Use a 23 kg (50 lb) line, a heavy 5/0 hook and bait of squid, octopus, fish or crab.

FIREFISH, RED

Pterois volitans
Also known as Butterfly Cod, Scorpion Cod, Zebrafish, Lionfish and Turkeyfish.

The firefish is spectacularly unusual, with a dazzling array of fins and spikes and splashes of colour. It belongs to the family of scorpion fish of which the red scorpion cod is a member. The body is zebra-striped in red and cream and the fins are creamy with numerous dark spots except on the spines. Rays of the dorsal and pectoral fins are unusually long and colourful and joined only by a very small membrane. The head is grotesque-looking with red fleshy growths about it.

The flesh is firm and white and good eating but overlooked when other fish are plentiful.

HABITAT AND GROWTH
It is a tropical species which grows to about 39 cm (15 in) and is usually seen in shallow water around coral reefs. This fish should be handled with care to avoid being stung by the dorsal spines which are poisonous but not deadly. A sting can cause great pain — even when the fish is dead.

FISHING
Occasionally caught when fishing for other species.

JEWFISH, LITTLE

Johnius amblycephalus
Also known as River Perch.

Its appearance is very similar to that of the mulloway and it is often thought to be a juvenile of that species. It is silvery above with a tinge of grey and a bright silvery belly. The inside of the mouth is a bright golden yellow similar to the teraglin.

The flesh is firm and good eating.

HABITAT AND GROWTH
It occurs in rivers and estuaries from the Queensland-New South Wales border to Rockhampton in Queensland where it attains a length of 30 cm (12 in).

FISHING
Prawns are the favoured bait. Use a 2/0 hook on a 4 kg (9 lb) line and rig no. 4 or 15.

MULLOWAY

Argyrosomus hololepidotus

For many years it was known as Jewfish, Jewie, and Soapy, names still being used.

It is grey-blue above, silver with a greenish tint on the sides, and silver underneath. It is very similar in appearance to teraglin,

except that the mulloway's tail fin is convex and the teraglin's is concave. The teraglin also has a very yellow mouth. Mulloway has a long, strong body and large scales.

The flesh is white, of good texture, and highly regarded.

HABITAT AND GROWTH

Mulloway occur from south Queensland to Bass Strait. It feeds on squid, octopus and a wide range of fish as well as beach worms, pipis and mussels. It ranges from deep offshore reefs to coastal beaches and rivers beyond the tidal influence. It grows as big as 59 kg (130 lb) and 2 m (6½ ft).

FISHING

The best catches are made in the hottest months of the year. January and February are by far the best months but catches are made almost all year round. Most large catches are made at dusk and up to three hours after dark. Small mulloway up to 3 kg (6 lb) are referred to as soapies, but they are also good eating.

Use only fresh bait, preferably live yellowtail, squid, mackerel fillet or mullet fillet. Suspend the bait about 1 m (3 ft) off the bottom, with a running ball sinker above the swivel to which is attached a 2 m (6½ ft) nylon trace. A 5 kg (11 lb) nylon line with a 3/0 hook would do for small fish but a 14 kg (30 lb) nylon line with an 8/0 hook is needed to handle larger fish. The smaller fish bite more freely during the day on fresh green prawn, beach worm, pipis and mussels. Use rig no. 4 or 15.

PERCH, GOLDEN

Macquaria ambigua

Also widely known as Callop, Yellowbelly and Murray Perch.

It is olive green above with golden sides and undersides, a single dorsal fin and a rounded tailfin.

Good eating, but sometimes has a muddy flavour.

HABITAT AND GROWTH

Native freshwater species found throughout the Murray-Darling system in most rivers and dams since restocking by the Inland Fisheries Research Station. A 24 kg (54 lb) golden perch was recorded from Kow Swamp, Victoria, but it was exceptional; the average fish caught is 1-2 kg (3-4 lb).

FISHING

It is a good fighter and in fast flowing streams, fish with a running sinker, using a 2/0 to 4/0 hook and a 6 kg (13 lb) line. Best baits are shrimp, yabbies, earthworms, grubs and mussels. After dark, use a float and have the bait about 1 m (3 ft) below the surface. Use rig no. 2, 4 or 17.

TUPONG

Pseudaphritis urvilli

Sometimes called a Freshwater Flathead or Congolli.

The tupong is muddy brown to greenish brown on the top with white below, mauve on the sides of the head with brown spots on the dorsal and tailfin. This fish is becoming scarce. Fair eating.

HABITAT AND GROWTH

Found in the coastal streams either fresh or salt, of South Australia, Victoria and Tasmania. It grows to 35 cm (14 in).

FISHING

Use a light 3.5 kg (8 lb) nylon line and a 2/0 short shanked hook and rig no. 20, 21 or 22. Shrimp is the best bait.

WHITING, ROCK
Haletta semifasciata

The male of this fish is generally a light silvery-brown with splotches of iridescent green-blue about the body, head and fins. The blue lines about the eye are similar to markings found on a maori wrasse. The caudal fin is slightly convexed and the snout is extended. The female has all brown tonings — dark above fading to light silvery-brown below with a few dark splotches.

The flesh is white and good eating.

HABITAT AND GROWTH
This fish is most abundant in shallow coastal waters near weedy and rocky areas. It is found along the southern coast from Western Australia to New South Wales and also in Tasmanian waters. It grows to 40 cm (16 in).

♂

♀

FISHING
Using a whiting rig no. 21, a light 4 kg (9 lb) line and a 6/0 hook. The best bait is sand and blood worm but a small peeled prawn or pipi will provide good results.

WIRRAH
Acanthistius ocellatus

Dark green with numerous black-rimmed blue spots scattered all over the body and fins. A short-bodied, robust fish with a large mouth. The skin is very thick.

The flesh is white but tough and not worth keeping. Most fish are returned to the sea.

HABITAT AND GROWTH
The wirrah is caught on the coast and nearby offshore reefs of southern Queensland and N.S.W. A related species *(A. serratus)* occurs in Western Australia. Grows to a length of 45 cm (18 in).

FISHING
This fish has particularly tough skin and puts up a good fight when hooked, although it's often referred to as 'an old boot'. Usually caught while fishing for other species.

WRASSE, HUMPHEAD MAORI
Cheilinus undulatus
Also known as Blue-Tooth Groper, Giant Wrasse and Double-Headed Parrot Fish.

It is a deep, powerful fish, with a long single dorsal fin and a long anal fin. The tailfin is rounded; colouring varies with age but all have a blue tint. The head has Maori markings of bright blue lines. It has large scales, each of which carries a red stripe. Adults develop a flesh protruberance that extends in front of the eyes on top of the head and gives rise to the name 'double header'.

Eating quality generally good, but varies with age.

HABITAT AND GROWTH
The humphead Maori wrasse is the largest member of the wrasse family and fish of 50 kg (110 lb) are fairly common. It inhabits northern coral reefs.

FISHING
Very heavy gear is needed even for small fish — 45 kg (100 lb) line, a size 8/0 or 10/0 hook and rig no. 9 or 16. Fish the bottom on the deep edge of a coral shelf. Any fish bait, hermit crab or prawn will be readily accepted.

CHAPTER FIVE

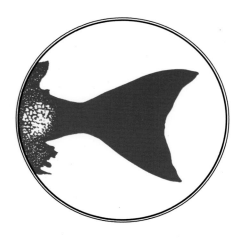

Fish with a Concave Tail Fin

BLUE-EYE
Hyperglyphe antarctica
Also known as Bream Trevalla

This is a heavy, robust fish, generally brownish with light-red tonings and darker blotches about the head and snout that fade on the back above the lateral line. It has five or six short spines preceding the dorsal filament. It has a large dark-blue eye with a bright yellow ring surrounding it. The caudal fin is forked.

The flesh is firm and white and good eating.

HABITAT AND GROWTH
The blue-eye grows to 140 cm (55 in) and can weigh in excess of 38 kg (83 lb). It is found in variable depths from 40 m to 900 m (131 ft to 2,960 ft) off the southern coast of Australia from New South Wales to Western Australia including Tasmania.

FISHING
This is a large deep water fish usually caught in trawl nets. They will take a whole fish bait, squid or large prawn. You need heavy gear, a 37 kg (80 lb) line an 8/0 hook and rig no. 16.

BOARFISH, BLACK SPOTTED
Zanclistius elevatus

The body is short and deep, silvery-grey in colour with broad vertical bands. It has a large eye and a protruding snout. The dorsal fin is particularly long and has a distinct black spot. The first six spines of the dorsal are very strong as are some of the rays of the ventral and anal fins.

It is good eating.

HABITAT AND GROWTH

This is a deep water specie found all along the bottom half of Australia and Tasmania where it grows to about 30 cm (12 in).

FISHING

Use any fish bait, squid or prawn. Usually caught by trawling. Rig no. 16 with a 3/0 hook.

BOARFISH, GIANT
Paristiopterus labiosus

Body elongate and compressed with a reddish-brown colouring and three distinct oblique dark stripes. The lower jaw is slightly longer than the upper. The body is covered with very small scales and the snout is concave from above the eye. There is a big change with age. The stripes disappear, the snout becomes more prominent and the fins take on a different shape.

The flesh is firm and white and very good to eat.

HABITAT AND GROWTH

Found all along the southern half of our continent including Tasmania where it grows to a length of at least 91 cm (36 in).

FISHING

The giant boarfish is caught when fishing offshore waters. Fish to 60 cm (24 in) are more common. They will take most fish baits, squid and octopus. They are bottom dwelling. Use a 14 kg (30 lb) line, a 4/0 hook and rig no. 16.

BOARFISH, YELLOW-SPOTTED
Paristiopterus gallipavo

It has a deep robust body with an extended blunt snout and rather large mouth. Colouring is pearly grey, the head and body suffused with pink. Entire body and fins with small yellow spots. The first 7 dorsal spines elongate. This is a good eating fish.

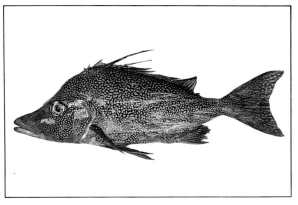

HABITAT AND GROWTH
The yellow-spotted boarfish prefers the colder waters of the coast of New South Wales, Victoria, Tasmania, South Australia and the southern half of Western Australia. It grows to about 91 cm (36 in).

FISHING
Rarely caught, it is usually taken when fishing for other species on wide offshore reefs; more often taken by trawlers.

BREAM, PIKEY
Acanthopagrus berda

The bronze body is robust and deep, with grey-green reflections, fading to a silvery belly. Similar to the black bream found in the southern half of the continent.

The flesh is firm and white and very good eating.

HABITAT AND GROWTH
This is a very common fish in the tropics where it attains a length of 55 cm (22 in) in Australian waters but much larger in Papua New Guinea. It lives in close inshore waters and in the estuaries and feeds on oysters, crustaceans and prawns.

FISHING
Caught in the same manner as the black bream down south. Fish

close to the shore at night with a light line about 4 kg (9 lb) and without a sinker if possible. If a small shot of lead is required it is best placed on the line as near to the hook as possible, otherwise use a running sinker and a one-metre trace. A 2/0 short shank hook will do for fish to 1 kg (2 lb) but a slightly heavier line and a 4/0 hook may be required for larger fish. Fish a rising tide for best results. Because this fish feeds in shallow waters, it can be scared by noise and flashing light. It's not a fussy eater and will take almost anything offered, including prawn, crab, mullet and mullet gut, and worms. The bait doesn't have to be very fresh.

BREAM, SLATE

Plectorhynchus pictus

Also known as Thicklip Bream, Bluey, Blackall, Painted Sweetlip and Morwong.

Juvenile slate bream are brown with golden tonings, with a number of dark bands running the length of the fish. Adult fish lose most of their colour and take on a dull grey-blue look, with small dark splotches all over the body. The tail is speckled with small olive-yellow spots.

Not as good to eat as emperor or coral trout, but the flesh is firm and acceptable.

HABITAT AND GROWTH

This fish is common in the tropics. It is found all along the Queensland coast, around the top half of the continent and the top half of Western Australia. It frequents sandy areas of the reef but will, on occasions, move into estuaries. It is usually found in large schools. They have been known to grow to 81 cm (32 in) and can weigh 4½ kg (10 lb).

FISHING

They will usually take any fish bait, prawn or crab. Fish the bottom using rig no. 16, a 14 kg (30 lb) line and a strong 4/0 hook.

BULLSEYE, RED

Priacanthus macracanthus

Also known as Bigeye.

It has large black eyes surrounded by deep red, and the fins are reddish. The scales are small and the body a bright pink. The fins

are blotched with dark spots and the mouth is bright orange. The body is short and deep, not unlike that of a nannygai.

Not particularly good eating as juveniles.

HABITAT AND GROWTH
Found right along the coast of Queensland and New South Wales where it lives in the shallow bays and creeks during winter and close offshore at other times. Grows to about 38 cm (15 in) but the average fish caught is about 25 cm (10 in).

FISHING
Caught mostly at night from wharves and jetties, using prawns or a strip of fish bait on a 2/0 hook and 5 kg (11 lb) line. Use rig no. 4.

CARP, GOLDEN
Carassius auratus

Also known as Goldfish and Prussian Carp.

Of European origin, it varies in colour from green to pink on top, with silvery sides and underbelly. Often used as live bait for Murray cod.

Poor quality table fish.

81

HABITAT AND GROWTH
Found in rivers in the southern half of Australia west of the Great Dividing Range. It prefers still water and weed beds. Not quite as common as other carp, but its habits are much the same, and it is extremely hardy. It reaches a maximum length of 33 cm (13 in), grows to about 2.2 kg (5 lb) but fish caught average about 23 cm (9 in). Breeds prolifically in spring and summer. It forages in weed patches for food and disturbs the mud, often causing an exodus of more important species of fish.

FISHING
Fish along the weed beds in still water with a quill float, 2½ kg (6 lb) nylon line and a no. 1 hook, and rig no. 2. Use worms, yabbies or shrimps.

DRUMMER, BLACK

Girella elevata

Shape resembles that of a luderick, but colouring is darker. Leaves something to be desired as a table fish.

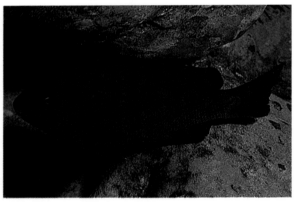

HABITAT AND GROWTH
The black drummer is found only on the New South Wales coast. Mainly weed-eating, with a fondness for deep water close to the rock foreshores where there is an ample supply of cabbage weed and cunjevoi and plenty of white surging water to dislodge it.

FISHING
Usually caught by rock fishermen who berley the gutters by kicking cabbage weed into the water and throwing bread in the wash. Has a small mouth, so a no. 6 extra strong hook is best. A bobby cork rig saves snagging and will get best results. Black drummer will take cunjevoi and a crust of bread as well as cabbage weed.

Drummer are especially strong swimmers, and when hooked dive for a rock crevice where they wedge themselves. They are a great sport fish but the best way to prepare for the table is to bleed them as soon as they are caught. Then fillet and skin them. Allow to soak in water for an hour or two. Use rig no. 17 or 28.

HUSSAR
Lutjanus amabilis

The hussar is a bright pink, with a yellow band along the lateral line. The caudal fin is pink. It is a member of the perch family, and its flesh is firm and good eating.

HABITAT AND GROWTH
This tropical fish is a reef-dweller usually caught when fishing for other species. It is a particularly strong swimmer and found from the Queensland — New South Wales border, north to Rockhampton. It grows to a length of 46 cm (18 in). The usual run of fish caught is around 2-3 kg (4½-7lb).

FISHING
A strong 4/0 to 6/0 hook on a 14 kg (30 lb) breaking strain line, using a snapper rig is best. Use rig no. 16.

KINGFISH, BLACK
Rachycentron canadum
Often referred to as a Cobia or Sergeant Fish.

Black kingfish is a recognised gamefish and a tenacious fighter. It is the shape of a yellowtail kingfish but with a flat head, a large mouth and a jutting lower jaw, and is black all over with brown and silvery bands running along the length of the body.

The flesh is white and good eating.

HABITAT AND GROWTH
It feeds at all depths on offshore reefs off southern Queensland, New South Wales and Western Australia at about the same latitude. The largest recorded black kingfish caught in Australian waters weighed 49.45 kg (109 lb). Fish 12 kg (26 lb) are more common.

FISHING
Most fish are caught by trolling with whole fish or a lure. Best baitfish is garfish, cowanyoung or pilchard. Many are caught with a bobby cork and a 16 kg (35 lb) nylon line with a trace about 6 m (20 ft) long and a 9/0 hook. Some fish are caught on the bottom when reef fishing. Use rigs no. 1, 5, 6, 12 or 17.

KNIGHT FISH

Cleidopus gloriamaris

Also known as Pineapple Fish, Port and Starboard.

The body is encased in an armour made up of small plates each of which has a pointed ridge, earning it the name of pineapple fish. It is bright yellow, each plate surrounded by a black border. The lips are black.

Knight fish should not be eaten.

HABITAT AND GROWTH
Found in the offshore waters of northern New South Wales and Queensland. Most fish caught are about 15 cm (6 in) long but they are known to attain a length of 28 cm (11 in).

FISHING
They are considered a trash fish and are usually hauled in by prawn trawlers working the offshore waters.

LONG-TOM, SLENDER
Strongylura leiura

Green on top with silvery sides, and a great fighter which leaps about like a small gamefish. Body long and slender, tail forked.
Slender long-tom makes good eating.

HABITAT AND GROWTH
Grows up to 1 m long in New South Wales and Queensland coastal waters and the tropical north; rarely seen around Tasmania or South Australia. Found around weedbeds when spawning.

FISHING
Will take a fish bait or prawn on a 1/0 hook. A light on the water at night when they are 'schooling' will attract them so much they will leap towards it. With a light from a lakatoy in the islands, fishermen say this species even leaped into the canoe, striking the sides so hard their sharp beaks have often become embedded in the timber. That can be dangerous! Use a 5 kg (11 lb) nylon line and rigs no. 23 or 29.

LONG-TOM, STOUT
Tylosurus macleayanus

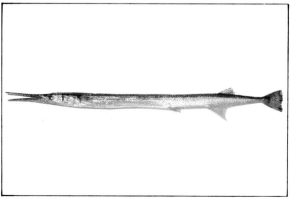

Green on top and silvery below. The largest and most common of the species around the Queensland and New South Wales border. Resembles the slender long-tom but is much stouter.

The stout long-tom makes good eating.

HABITAT AND GROWTH
This species is most common in Queensland and northern New South Wales, where it grows up to 120 cm (47 in) and weighs 3 kg (6 lb). It is mostly seen in the open sea.

FISHING
Will take a lure trolled at about 5 knots on a strip of fish bait. Use a 7 kg (15 lb) line, a 2/0 hook and rig no. 3, 4 or 23.

LUDERICK

Girella tricuspidata

Commonly known as Blackfish but often referred to as Nigger or Darkie.

It is brownish on the back and lighter below with up to 12 narrow vertical dark bands on the side. It looks bronze when caught off the seafront and for a short time after entering the estuary. Fish caught further up the estuaries lose the bronze look.

The flesh of fish from this area sometimes has a weedy taste. Otherwise it is choice food.

HABITAT AND GROWTH
Grows up to 70 cm (27 in) and weighs as much as 4 kg (9 lb) but those usually caught are between 0.5 and 1 kg (1-2 lb). It spawns in the mouths of estuaries and surf during autumn in the southern waters and later moves to shallow weedy flats or around weed-covered rocks, piles or fallen trees.

FISHING
Largely vegetarian and in the sheltered waters of rivers and bays, luderick are always fished for with green weed. On the ocean front they prefer the sea lettuce or cabbage that grows profusely on the ocean rock front. A berley of chopped weed mixed with sand and perhaps a little pollard is a great attraction.

Most people use a long light rod about 3.5 m (11 ft) long, a 2.5 kg (6 lb) breaking strain line, a light float and a no. 6 blackfish hook and rig no. 31. The weed is wound around the hook, and

must cover the whole of the shank, leaving a tail of about 6 cm
(2½ in).

MACKEREL, FRIGATE
Auxis thazard

Body elongate and robust with a large mouth and small teeth,
two widely separated dorsal fins, the second much smaller than
the first which is usually standing upright. There are six to eight
small fins behind the second fin. The caudal fin is forked. Dark
blue above, silvery below, with numerous wavy markings running
across the top half of the body.

The flesh is strong and poor eating.

HABITAT AND GROWTH
Prefers warm waters and is seldom found south of lat. 36°S. It
grows to a length of 46 cm (18 in) and weight of about 1.4 kg (3
lb). It is a surface fish and feeds on other smaller fish.

FISHING
Not especially fished for, and when caught while fishing for
other fish are used as bait or returned to the sea.

MANGROVE JACK
Lutjanus argentimaculatus
Also known as Dog Bream, Purple Sea Perch, Red
Bass, Red Perch and Creek Red Bream.

Colour varies from pink to reddish brown with each scale
carrying a spot that forms into longitudinal lines. It has strong
powerful teeth. It is a member of the perch family.

It is a delicious table fish but unfortunately it is often confused
with red bass, which is known to have been the cause of
ciguatera poisoning and is not accepted for sale to fish markets.
The two fish are easy to distinguish because the scales of the
mangrove jack can easily be dislodged, whereas the scales on the
red bass are very difficult to remove.

HABITAT AND GROWTH
As the name implies, mangrove jack is a fish that is found in

estuaries and bays where mangroves exist along the tropical coast of Queensland, Western Australia and the Top End. It can attain a growth of 16 kg (35 lb) but the average fish caught weighs about 3 kg (6 lb).

FISHING

Mangrove jack is a strong fighter and has a good array of teeth necessitating the use of a wire trace on a line about 7 kg (15 lb) breaking strain and a 4/0 or 5/0 hook. Bait can be squid, octopus, prawn, mullet strip or small live baitfish. You can fish with or without a float, but it will make a more attractive bait and covers more territory. Use rig no. 10 or 17.

MULLET, YELLOW-EYE
Aldrichetta forsteri

The colouring of the many species of mullet is similar, but this one is olive green on top, sometimes with a brown tint, silvery green sides and silver below. The head is broad and rounded. This species has a yellow eye as the name implies, and no eyelid.

Yellow-eye mullet makes good eating.

HABITAT AND GROWTH

It prefers the colder waters and ranges from southern New South Wales to Fremantle in Western Australia, including Tasmania.

It is particularly plentiful in Victoria and South Australia. Yellow-eye mullet grows to a maximum length of about 35 cm (14 in) and weight of 500 g (1 lb). Most fish caught are about 30 cm (12 in) long.

FISHING
It feeds on plankton but will readily take a small bait of oyster, peeled prawn, bread or dough, especially if berleyed with a mixture of bread, pollard and bran. Use a very light 2-3 kg (5-7 lb) line with a very small sinker, if any, and a no. 10 short-shanked hook. Use rig no. 2 or 29.

PERCH, MOSES
Lutjanus russelli
Also known as Red Bream, Fingermark Bream, or Russell's Snapper.

A black spot on the sides just above the lateral line helps identify the Moses perch. The general colour of the fish varies with age from a light red to a bronze, similar to the colouring of a snapper, with about six golden stripes running along the body. They are more prominent on larger fish.

The flesh is white and firm and it is considered one of our better table fish.

HABITAT AND GROWTH
It is found along the entire Queensland coast, the Northern Territory and down the northern half of the coast of Western Australia. It inhabits the inshore reefs when young, but the deeper reefs offshore when older. It is bottom feeding and grows to a length of 51 cm (20 in).

FISHING
It will readily take most fish baits, prawns and other shellfish. The average run of fish is about 38 cm (15 in) and a 14 kg (30 lb) line with a 4/0 to 6/0 hook will suffice. Use rig no. 9 or 16.

PERCH, ORANGE
Anthias pulchellus
Also known as Black Spot Perch.

This is a very colourful fish with orange-red tonings, light orange fins, a dark eye and a conspicuous jet black splotch about half

89

way along the dorsal fin, this fin has 24 sharp spiny filaments. The caudal fin is concave.

The flesh is firm and white and highly regarded as a table fish.

HABITAT AND GROWTH
This fish ranges the entire bottom half of Australia and Tasmania where it grows to 36 cm (14 in). It is a reef dweller found in depths ranging from 60 m to 160 m (197 ft to 526 ft).

FISHING
It is usually caught when reef fishing for snapper. A 3/0 hook is large enough on a 14 kg (30 lb) line and rig no. 16. Bait can be prawn, crab, squid or a small piece of fresh fish bait.

PERCH, SCARLET SEA
Lutjanus malabaricus
Also known as Red Snapper, Red Jew, Red Emperor, Nannygai and Red Bream.

This is a deep red fish all over, somewhat similar to a true red emperor without the darker shades. The anal fin has 8 or 9 rays whereas the emperor has 10 or 11.

The flesh is firm and white and highly rated as a table fish.

HABITAT AND GROWTH
This species occurs in and around the coral reefs of Queensland and Western Australia where it can attain a growth of 14 kg (30 lb).

FISHING
Scarlet sea perch is a strong fighter and will take any respectable fish bait, crab or prawn. Use a strong 6.0 hook, a 14 kg (30 lb) line and rig no. 9 or 16.

PERCH, SILVER
Bidyanus bidyanus

This native freshwater fish varies in colour from bright silver to blackish. Juveniles may be mottled. It is bred at the Inland Fisheries Research Station at Narrandera, New South Wales, for widespread distribution. Often referred to as a grunter because of the noise it makes when captured.

It has a small mouth and is a fairly popular food.

HABITAT AND GROWTH
Silver perch is widely distributed in inland waters. It likes to hide under fallen trees in deeper water and bites more freely at night. It grows to 4.5 kg (10 lb) but the average fish caught weigh 1 to 1.5 kg (2-3 lb). A silver perch tagged near Narrandera, New South Wales, in 1969 when it weighed 1.3 kg (3 lb) was caught seven years and 203 days later; it had travelled 70 km (43 miles) upriver and weighed only 200 g (7 oz) more.

FISHING
Best baits are shrimps, crickets, earthworms and yabbies. Use 4 kg (9 lb) nylon, a light float and a nylon trace about 46 cm (18 in) long with a no. 4 to no. 1 hook. Use rig no. 2.

PERCH, STRIPED SEA
Lutjanus vittus

Also known as a Hussar and Yellow-banded Sea Perch.

This fish is bright pink all over fading towards the belly. The dark band about mid-way running from the gills to the tail is a distinguishing feature. The fins are bright yellow sometimes edged in red. It is very similar to a hussar but is distinguished

91

from this fish by its 10 dorsal spines, one less than the hussar.
  The flesh is white and firm and very good eating.

HABITAT AND GROWTH
It is common on the coastal reefs off Queensland where it grows
to 38 cm (15 in). It is bottom feeding.

FISHING
They are usually caught when fishing for other bottom-dwelling
species such as emperor and cod.

SALMON, QUINNAT
Oncorhynchus tschawytscha

Elongated body reminiscent of its salmonid cousin the trout.
Olive green to reddish-brown on the upper body, but a lighter
silvery colour below. Around spawning time the adults are an
overall silver colour. They often have a mottled pattern on the
back, a little like Murray cod, or numerous small black spots on
the back and top of the tail.
  Excellent food fish.

HABITAT AND GROWTH
Confined to Lakes Purrumbete and Bullen Merri, south-west of

Melbourne. First attempts to introduce them into Victoria and Tasmania were made in 1874, but it was not until 1977 that biologists achieved success. In the US and New Zealand they mature at sea and run back into fresh water to spawn, but the pattern did not emerge in Australia. Spawning is still a problem, but an extensive research and breeding programme at Snobs Creek Hatchery near Eildon looks like being able to keep up stocks in the two lakes. The fish feed on galaxis (minnows) and previous stocking attempts produced fish of up to 9 kg (19 lb).

FISHING
Seasons are strictly controlled, and in the early years the fish would strike at anything, even cigarette butts tossed into the water. Trolling from a dinghy is the most popular method, and the fish are great fighters. Rainbow trout tackle is ideal.

SNAPPER, LONG-SPINED
Argyrops spinifer
Also known as Fryingpan Snapper.

A close relative of the snapper family but readily distinguished by its much deeper body and long dorsal spines. The colouring is similar to the snapper, reddish pink shading to silvery below with four or five dark reddish bands about the fish which become fainter with age.
 The flesh is flaky and white and very good eating.

HABITAT AND GROWTH
It ranges the entire Queensland coast where it attains a length of 50 cm (20 in). It is bottom feeding.

FISHING
It is caught on reefs and coral on the Barrier Reef with a 4/0 hook on a 24 kg (50 lb) line, rig no. 16. It is not a fussy eater and will take most fish baits, squid, crab, etc.

SUCKER FISH, SLENDER
Echineis naucrates

An elongate fish, dark brown with a broad black band running the length of the head and body. A powerful sucking disc is situated on the head.

Slender sucker fish is not usually eaten.

HABITAT AND GROWTH
It uses the sucking disc to hitch a ride on larger fish, usually sharks. It will detach itself at will to feed. It is abundant all along the Queensland coast.

FISHING
It is often caught when bottom fishing for other species but never especially sought after.

TENCH
Tinca tinca

The body is elongate, generally the shape of European carp with a short, single dorsal fin which is high and close to the middle of the fish. The pectoral fins are large and low on the body. The tail fin is robust, making the tench a powerful swimmer. Colour is variable, depending on locale, but basically is an olive to dark grey above and slightly fading below to a light grey. It has a small mouth with a small barbel each side.

The flesh is quite edible but tench is not one of our best table fish.

HABITAT AND GROWTH

Tench is a freshwater species of European origin. It is a powerful but sluggish fish and found in clear fast-flowing streams as well as muddy backwaters. It attains a length of at least 72 cm (28 in) and weight to 9 kg (20 lb) in Australia but has been known to grow much larger in Europe. Spawning occurs in spring and early summer, the eggs attaching to plants and hatching in about 7 days. It feeds mainly on the larvae of insects, yabbies, shrimps and vegetable matter.

FISHING

It is not a fussy eater. As the average fish is 500 g-2 kg (1-5 lb), a light rod, 5 kg (11 lb) line and a no. 4 hook is all that's needed. Use rig no. 2 or 21. Preferred bait is worms, yabbies or snails.

TERAGLIN

Atractoscion aequidens
Also known as Trag.

A relative of the mulloway family with which it is often confused. The colouring and shape are similar, but the scales are smaller and the inside of the mouth has a reddish-grey appearance. Also, the tailfin is slightly concave, in contrast to the mulloway's convex tail.

The flesh is rather soft and bruises easily, but is rated a good table fish.

HABITAT AND GROWTH

Found only off the NSW and southern Queensland coasts, usually over offshore reefs and gravel beds at any depth on the Continental Shelf. Grows to around 11 kg (25 lb) but the average

caught is 2 to 4 kg (5 to 10 lb). It is nocturnal, but often caught at first light and dusk.

FISHING

Big catches can be expected when they are biting, but it is essential to keep a bait or fish with the school. In other words, if all strike together one angler should leave his fish swimming with the school until the others have landed their fish and rebaited before attempting to haul in. When biting freely they will often rise to the bait. You need about a 7-9 kg (15-20 lb) line and a 5/0 hook baited with squid, mullet, prawn, bonito, yellowtail or pilchard. Use rigs no. 14 or 15.

TROUT, BROOK
Salvelinus fontinalis

The brook trout resembles the brown and rainbow trout. The top half of the body is heavily marked with yellow, green and whitish patterns against a green background. The abdomen of the male is orange in breeding season. The dorsal fin has numerous dark lines, all other fins are orange with a dark margin. It has a large mouth and is a strong fighter when hooked.

The brook trout is good eating.

HABITAT AND GROWTH
A native of North America, it was introduced into Tasmanian streams in the early 1900s and later into New South Wales. It is found also in South Australian streams, usually growing to about 53 cm (21 in).

FISHING
Use a fly rod, tapered line and leader for dry and wet flies and longtails; spinning rod and reel for lures. When bait fishing use a light rod and reel, 3 kg (6 lb) line and shrimp, earthworms, crickets, grasshoppers, beetles or wood grubs. Use rigs no. 20, 21 or 22.

Caution: Check local trout fishing laws before wetting a line.

TROUT, BROWN
Salmo trutta

As the name implies, brown trout is predominantly light brown, with dark spots on the sides and back. The lower spots are encircled with red. The dorsal fin is spotted.

This fish makes good eating.

HABITAT AND GROWTH
This species was introduced to Australia from Great Britain in 1864. Tasmania was first to have them but now they can be found in freshwater lakes, dams and streams in all States except Queensland and the far north. The largest brown trout caught in Australia weighed 13 kg (29 lb) but most fish caught weigh about 500 g to 1 kg (1-2 lb).

FISHING
Use a fly rod, tapered line and leader for dry and wet flies and longtails; spinning rod and reel for lures. If bait fishing, use a

light rod and reel, 3 kg (7 lb) line with shrimp, earthworms, crickets, grasshoppers, beetles and wood grubs. Use rig no. 2, 21 or 22.

Caution: Check your State's laws on trout fishing before you wet a line.

TROUT, CORAL

Plectropomus leopardus
Also known as Leopard Fish.

Range in colour from pink to red to brown, but the small blue spots over the body and head are a common feature.

The firm white flesh is delicious.

Sometimes confused with the coral cod, *Cephalopholis miniatus*, which has similar markings. The trout has an inward-curved tail and 7 or 8 spines in the first dorsal; the cod has a rounded tail and nine spines in the first dorsal. The coral trout is a protogynous hermaphrodite, that is, the individual becomes sexually mature as a female and then later in life changes its sex to become a male. It is thus one sex at a time and cannot self-fertilise. Most coral trout mature as females when they are about 22 cm (9 in) long and about 2 years old. These females remain reproductive until they are 3 to 4 years old. During this time their ovaries average about 4.5 per cent of their total weight and a 2-year-old can produce 83 000 eggs a year, a 4-year-old about 458 000 eggs a year.

HABITAT AND GROWTH
Coral trout are widely dispersed around coral reef waters of Queensland, the Northern Territory and Western Australia. They grow to about 110 cm (43 in) and weigh more than 20 kg (44 lb).

FISHING
Use a 23 kg (50 lb) line with a 5/0 or 6/0 hook and rig no. 16. A fillet of any recognised baitfish is readily taken.

TROUT, RAINBOW
Salmo gairdnerii

Colours vary according to environment. A broad red stripe runs lengthwise along the sides of the male, the fish is blue-green above and white below and a number of dark spots all over, except the belly.
    Excellent eating.

HABITAT AND GROWTH
A native of California, USA, it was introduced to our waters from New Zealand in 1894. It can now be found in all States except Queensland and the far north. It prefers fast, turbulent

water. The world record stands at 16.78 kg (37 lb) but the average fish caught weighs 500 g to 1 kg (1 to 2 lb).

FISHING
Use a fly rod, tapered line and leader for dry and wet flies and longtails; spinning rod and reel for lures. If bait fishing, use a light rod and reel, a 3 kg (6 lb) line with shrimp, earthworms, crickets, grasshoppers, beetles and wood grubs. Use rigs no. 20, 21 or 22.

Caution: Check the State's trout fishing laws before you wet a line.

TUSK-FISH, BLUE
Choerodon schoenleinii
Also known as Venus Tusk-fish.

If you have visited Heron Island or the true coral reefs on the Great Barrier Reef you are likely to have seen this fish in pools when the tide receded. It is an attractive fish of many colours; generally greenish-blue with some iridescent blue and red streaks and spots around the snout. The dorsal fin is also heavily marked with Maori lines.

It is not rated highly as a table fish, but the flesh is firm and white and can be quite palatable.

HABITAT AND GROWTH
The blue tusk-fish attains a weight of 8 kg (18 lb) and a length of 72 cm (28 in). The average fish caught is about 1 to 3 kg (2-7 lb). Blue tusk-fish lives in the shallow coral pools of the tropics.

FISHING
It can easily be netted in the coral pools at low tide or caught at any time with a handline, using a strong 1/0 or 2/0 hook and a 14 kg (30 lb) line. It will take most fish baits and crab. Use rig no. 9.

TUSK-FISH, VENUS

Choerodon venustus
Also known as Blue Parrot, Blue Spotted Groper, Parrot Fish, Pink Tusk Fish.

Colour is variable, ranging from green to a bright red. The head and body are covered with small blue spots. The strong teeth are curved. Venus tusk fish is a robust fish able to generate great power with its strong caudal fin.

The flesh is white, firm and flaky and good eating.

HABITAT AND GROWTH
Very abundant in the tropical north in the vicinity of offshore coral reefs where they attain a length of 48 cm (19 in) and a weight exceeding 3 kg (7 lb).

FISHING
Will readily take prawn, soldier crab and any fresh cut up fish bait. Use a 14 kg (30 lb) line and strong 4/0 hook and rig no. 16.

CHAPTER SIX

Fish with a Moderate Fork

BASS, AUSTRALIAN

Percalates colonorum

Also known as Australian Perch and Estuary Perch.

The Australian bass is olive-green above, with a golden belly and a reddish-tinted head. Fish from faster-running water are usually considerably slimmer than those taken from more placid water.

An excellent native sportfish, it is delicious to eat, although its numbers have dwindled to the stage where anglers usually keep few fish, returning most alive to the water.

HABITAT AND GROWTH

This native freshwater fish is found in rivers and streams to the tidal influence in southern Queensland from Tin Can Bay and throughout New South Wales, Victoria, South Australia and Tasmania. An occasional 3 kg (6 lb) fish is caught, but the average adult is about 1 kg (2 lb). It likes the protection of a fallen tree. The construction of dams and weirs has made bass scarce, as the structures interfere with its spawning run.

FISHING

It seems to bite more freely at dusk and after dark. Use a light rod and reel and 3 kg (6 lb) nylon line with a 1/0 hook, a quill float and just enough split shot to hold it under. Best baits are grasshoppers, crickets, worms and shrimps. Use rig no. 2 to no. 7 or 8. It will readily take an artificial lure, is a splendid striker and fights well.

BREAM, BLACK

Acanthopagrus butcheri

Also known as Silver Bream, Surf Bream, Southern Bream and Sea Bream.

The body is deep and robust and covered with scales. Black bream is generally silvery olive green with yellowish reflections. Bream taken from the sea are lighter in colour than those caught in the estuary especially in muddy habitats. They are then often referred to as silver bream and considered to be a different species.

They have white, tender flesh and are rated as one of our best table fish.

HABITAT AND GROWTH
Black bream are found along the coast of southern Western Australia, South Australia, Tasmania, Victoria, New South Wales and southern Queensland. They grown to 55 cm (22 in). They are a coastal species found along surfing beaches, in river mouths and estuaries feeding on shellfish, worms, crustaceans and small fish. They have strong teeth and are sometimes a pest to oyster farmers.

FISHING
The bream is probably the most common of marine fishes taken by anglers. Fishing is best after dark, usually on the last half of a rising tide with a light 3 kg (6 lb) line, a 1/0 or 2/0 short shank hook. Do not use a sinker unless it is absolutely necessary and then a small split shot right up close to the hook. They are not fussy eaters and will take almost any known bait including pudding mix and cheese. However most favoured bait is live yabby and prawn. Mullet and luderick gut is also popular. It is important to cover the hook completely and be gentle at the first approach bite. Allow the line to be taken across the fingers without restriction for about 1 m (3 ft) before closing the fingers on the line.

BREAM, IODINE
Gymnocranius bitorquatus
Also known as Collared Sea Bream, Sand Snapper, Pale-faced Bream, Coral Bream.

A brilliant silvery fish with golden reflections bearing irregular dark blotches that fade after death. All fins are golden yellow with a fleck of red. A distinguishing feature is the pale broad band across the back above and behind the eyes. It closely resembles a black bream.
Some fish have an iodine taste, hence the name. But not all fish are affected and when not evident the flesh has excellent table qualities.

HABITAT AND GROWTH
They frequent cays of the Great Barrier Reef and are found all along the Queensland coast, where they attain a length of 40 cm (16 in).

FISHING

They will take most any fish bait, prawn or pudding mix. Fish light as you would for black bream, but upgrade the line to 5 kg (11 lb) because of the proximity of the coral, and the likelihood of it being cut.

BREAM, THREADFIN

Nemipterus hexodon

Also known as Red Bream

Closely resembling the whiptail without the long trailing filament on the caudal fin. It is a reddish-pink all over with silvery tonings.

The flesh is firm and white and larger specimens are well worth eating.

HABITAT AND GROWTH

It is found all around the top half of Australia near coral. It grows to about 24 cm (9 in), and is frequently taken by prawn trawlers.

FISHING

The butterfly bream is a small fish that inhabits areas where

larger fish are readily taken, therefore it is not especially fished for. A 1/0 hook is all you need with a 4 kg (10 lb) line and a small lead shot near the hook. Prawn is a very acceptable bait.

BREAM, YELLOWFIN
Acanthopagrus australis
Also known as Silver Bream, Surf Bream, Sea Bream, Black Bream.

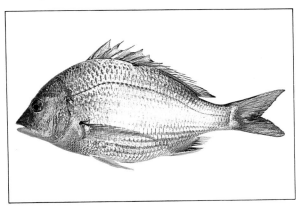

The body is deep and robust and covered with large scales. The back and sides are bronze with greenish tinges. The belly and jaw are white and the head has tints of blue and purple.

Its white, firm and tender flesh is rated as one of Australia's best table fish.

HABITAT AND GROWTH
Found along the coast of southern Western Australia, South Australia, Tasmania, Victoria and New South Wales. Primarily a bottom-feeding fish, it lives on shellfish, worms, prawns, crabs and yabbies. Grows to a length of 53 cm (21 in) but those caught are usually between 22 and 25 cm (9-10 in).

FISHING
Best fishing is at night on the last half of the rising tide, fishing close to shore. Cast the line away from the boat towards the shore. Do not use a sinker unless it is absolutely necessary, and then only a tiny shot close to the shank of the hook. The fish are timid and easily frightened on bright moonlight nights, so anchor quietly and do not flash a torch on the water or the shore. The bait must cover the hook entirely. A bream usually mouths the bait and plays with it. Any resistance on the line scares the fish. Allow the fish to run about a metre (3 ft) before you tighten your fingers on the line. The best baits are prawns, yabbies, mullet gut and worms. Use a 2½-3½ kg (6-8 lb) line with a 1/0 short shank hook. The line is best wound on to a cork cylinder so it can be laid against the side of the boat. Use rig no. 13 or no. 4 when fishing an ocean beach.

CARP, EUROPEAN
Cyprinus carpio
Also known as Mirror Carp and Calico Carp.

Introduced to Australian rivers and streams in 1876 and now a pest in rivers west of the Great Dividing Range. It disturbs the muddy bottom as it forages for food and it is said by many to deplete the stocks of indigenous fish such as Murray cod and perch. Similar in appearance and colouring to a relative, the crucian carp, except that it has fleshy whiskers beneath the mouth.

The table qualities are poor, as they are bony and the flesh is coarse and tastes muddy.

HABITAT AND GROWTH
Distribution is throughout Victoria, New South Wales, Tasmania, South Australia and southern parts of Queensland. It grows to a maximum weight of 7 kg (15 lb). The floods in 1976 were largely responsible for its wide distribution, and each subsequent flood widens it. The European carp prefers still waters near weedbeds.

FISHING
European carp will take most bait, but prefers shrimps, yabbies, worms and mussels. Use a quill float, about 4 kg (9 lb) nylon line and a 1/0 hook, enough split shot to balance the float, and rig no. 2.

DHU-FISH, WESTERN AUSTRALIAN
Glaucosoma hebraicum

This fish is almost identical to the pearl perch (*Glaucosoma scapulare*). The colouring is similar but the dhu-fish has a shade more brown marble tonings and the male of the species has an elongated soft dorsal ray. It is indeed difficult to tell them apart.

The eating quality of both is superb. Many in fact believe they are our best tablefish. The correct name of both fish is pearl perch but as the name dhu-fish is so widely used we have chosen this name as a heading for easy identification with appropriate cross references.

HABITAT AND GROWTH
Usually caught when fishing the offshore reefs for snapper between Shark Bay and Cape Naturaliste, Western Australia. It grows to 27 kg (60 lb).

FISHING
Prefers a live pilchard (mulie), small mullet, squid, or octopus. Use 4/0-8/0 hook and a 20 kg (45 lb) line and rig no. 16.

DRUMMER, SILVER
Kyphosus sydneyanus

Deep-bodied, with a small mouth. The colouring is silver on the upper body with prominent longitudinal bands. The under-body is greyish. In the southern States, where the average fish caught is much larger than in the eastern States, it is sometimes referred to as buffalo bream.

In New South Wales, where it is particularly sought, silver drummer is not considered as good to eat as the black drummer, particularly the larger fish.

HABITAT AND GROWTH
The silver drummer grows to about 76 cm (30 in) and 10 kg (22 lb) but the average fish caught is around 3.5 kg (8 lb). It lives along the rocky foreshores of all the southern States.

FISHING
Caught in deep holes by rock fishermen, usually with a rod, reel

107

and float — a rig similar to that used for luderick, but heavier. Hooks range from no. 4 to 10 extra strong and the line is usually about 11 kg (24 lb) on a good rod and a 15 cm (6 in) reel. Use rig no. 17 or 28.

EMPEROR, RED

Lutjanus sebae
Also known as King Snapper and Government Bream.

Adult fish are reddish and juveniles have three dark bands around the body. They're sometimes referred to as government bream because the bands are supposed to resemble the broad arrow once used to mark government stores. As the fish reach maturity the bands fade and become an attractive deep pink with pearly scales.

It is an excellent table fish.

HABITAT AND GROWTH
This much sought-after bottom-feeding species frequents tropical reefs, where it grows to 21 kg (48 lb).

FISHING
Caught by handline in the deeper channels around coral reefs, with almost any fish bait. However, it prefers prawn, squid and octopus. Use a 6/0 hook, 22 kg (50 lb) nylon line and rig no. 16.

EMPEROR, RED-FINNED

Lethrinus laticaudus

The reticulated emperor is grey-green with seven or eight light vertical bands. The fins are light pink and the base of the anal, pectoral and vertical fins are tinted red. The inside of the mouth is deep red.

The flesh is firm and white and very good eating.

HABITAT AND GROWTH
It is common in the warmer waters of Queensland, Northern Territory and Western Australia, around coral reefs where it can grow to 41 cm (16 in).

FISHING

It is caught when fishing for reef fish using 4/0 or 5/0 hook and prawn, fish or crustaceans. Use rig no. 16. and a 23 kg (50 lb) line.

EMPEROR, SPANGLED
Lethrinus nebulosus

This handsome fish is fairly easy to recognise by the scales, which all carry a blue spot in the centre, and by the top lip and inside of the mouth, which are bright orange. The fins are pale yellow on the trailing edge with splotches of light blue.

The flesh is white and highly rated for the table.

HABITAT AND GROWTH

Spangled Emperor inhabits the tropical coral reefs and cays where it grows to a length of at least 86 cm (34 in).

FISHING

A fairly common fish to catch as it will take most fish baits. They are bottom-feeding fish and strong fighters. Use an 18 kg (40 lb) line, 5/0 or 6/0 hooks and rig no. 16.

109

EMPEROR, SWEETLIP
Lethrinus chrysostomus

Olive green on top, silvery white below with dark vertical bands across the body. The head is reddish and the dorsal fin bright red. The bands disappear at death. The inside of the mouth is red. Shaped like a bream.

Flesh is white, flaky, and a delicate flavour some class as the best-tasting on the Barrier Reef.

HABITAT AND GROWTH
Most abundant of the emperor family, and found along the Queensland coast, especially on the Barrier Reef. The average fish caught is around 2 kg (4½ lb) but they do grow to as much as 10 kg (22 lb).

FISHING
Takes a bait freely and fights strongly when hooked, but must be hauled in quickly to avoid cut-offs on the coral. Use a 4/0 hook on a 15 kg (35 lb) line, rig no. 16. Not a fussy eater, and will readily take most fish baits, prawn, squid and octopus.

GALAXIAS, SPOTTED MOUNTAIN
Galaxias truttaceus

Also known as Mountain Trout, a misleading title discouraged by taxonomists.

The body is long and slender. The single dorsal fin is far back on the tail above the ventral fin. The anal fin is near the middle of the fish. The colouring is olive, dotted all over with dark spots and has a narrow dark band running the full length of the body. There is an oblique dark bar through the eye and two vertical bars above the pectoral fin.

It is not large enough to make an enjoyable meal.

HABITAT AND GROWTH
This species is found only in Tasmania, Victoria and South Australia, in clear, cool mountain streams. It is not a common fish and reaches a length only of about 15 cm (6 in).

FISHING
Occasionally caught when fishing for other species.

HARDYHEAD

Pranesus ogilbyi

A hardyhead is pale brown above and white below with a conspicuous silver streak along its side. It has a bony head and tough scales.
It is a baitfish.

HABITAT AND GROWTH
The hardyhead occurs in coastal bays, estuaries and harbours all along the eastern coast. It grows to 17 cm (6 in) but most fish are about 10 cm (4 in).

FISHING
These fish are caught for bait only. At night they are attracted to a bright light and will come to the surface where they can be easily netted. Use a fine mesh net such as is used for prawning.

111

MULLET, BLUESPOT GREY

Valamugil seheli

Also known as Black-spot Mullet, Blue-tailed Mullet, Long-armed Mullet, Long-finned Mullet and Sand Mullet.

Elongate and robust, with a more pointed head than most other mullet. The body is bright silver, greenish above, with a bright, light blue caudal fin. The dorsal is soft, the pectoral fins are yellow with a prominent blue-black spot at their base.

Quite a good food fish.

HABITAT AND GROWTH

The largest of the Queensland mullet, it grows to 11 kg (24 lb) and specimens of 3.5 to 4.5 kg (8 to 10 lb) are common. It's a northern estuary and inlet fish, rarely venturing much further south than Fraser Island, but particularly abundant in the Wide Bay area and Princess Charlotte Bay.

FISHING

Usually taken in arrowhead traps or in the course of netting other species.

MULLET, FLAT TAIL

Liza argentea

Also known as Jumping Mullet and Fan-tail Mullet.

This species is light brown above, silvery below. Scales are fairly large for size of fish and it has five rows of scales on the cheeks.

Mullet are an oily fish. Some people rave about them as food fish, others not.

HABITAT AND GROWTH

It is very common in estuaries of Western Australia, South Australia, Victoria, New South Wales, Queensland and Northern Territory. It attains a length of 30 cm (12 in). In quiet estuarine waters they can often be heard jumping at night and early morning.

FISHING

They are not easily enticed to take a bait. Use a luderick rig and fish about 50 cm (20 in) below the surface using no. 8 black fish

hook and a very light float. Entice them about with bread and use dough for bait. Sometimes a piece of meat will be their fancy. Other times small worms are successful. It's a case of trial and error.

MULLET, SEA

Mugil cephalus
Also known as River Mullet, Poddy Mullet, Bully Mullet and Hardgut Mullet.

Probably our most common edible fish. The sea mullet is olive green above with silvery sides and a tint of green and silver

below. The head is broad and rounded.

The flesh of the sea mullet is excellent table food. It can be grilled, fried or smoked. Most of the smoked roe available in shops is from sea mullet.

HABITAT AND GROWTH

During April and May, the adult fish congregate in the estuaries in preparation for migration to spawning areas in warmer waters. During the migration huge schools move close to beaches

113

and 3-5 km (2-3 miles) to seaward. Then and during winter, the females, which far outnumber the males, are full of roe. Towards spring, the fish return to the estuaries and continue upstream into brackish water where they may be seen jumping about, especially in the early hours of the morning. They are plentiful in all States except Tasmania. Sea mullet grow to a length of about 80 cm (31 in) but the average fish caught at sea is about 1 kg (2 lb) and 45 cm (18 in).

FISHING

Not generally caught by amateur fishermen, as they seldom take a bait except when they are in the estuaries. They live on minute matter such as plankton and oyster eggs. Sometimes they can be enticed to take a tiny bait of worm, oyster, bread, dough or peeled prawns, especially if berleyed with a mixture of bread, pollard and bran. When all else fails, try a small piece of curried suet. To catch a sea mullet on a baited hook other than in an estuary is almost impossible. Some are caught with a jag, but that is illegal. In the estuaries, try a no. 1 hook on a very light 2-3 kg (5-7 lb) line with no sinker, and cast out about 3 m from the boat or bank of the river. Use rig no. 21, 23 or 29.

PERCH, ENGLISH REDFIN
Perca fluviatilis

The redfin, or English perch, is a freshwater fish regarded by many as a nuisance and by others as a magnificent fighting fish. Australian conditions seem to suit this prolific breeder, and some scientists believe it played a major part in depleting our native fish population. It has a greenish back, white underside with 5 or 6 dark vertical bars. The dorsal fin is charcoal, the other fins are red.

Good eating once it is out of the juvenile stage.

HABITAT AND GROWTH

Found in many streams and canals, especially in the Murray and

Darling River systems. The growth rate is extremely rapid. A fish around 1.5 kg to 2 kg (3-5 lb) is the usual run of the school. The largest redfin caught in Australia weighed 10.43 kg (23 lb).

FISHING

It will readily take a lure, particularly the ABU Sonette, Super Duper, Flopy and small Wonder Wobbler. Troll about 15 m (50 ft) behind a boat travelling at 3 knots or a little slower. It will also readily take such bait as worms, yabbies, grubs and shrimps. Fish baits are also acceptable, but not preferred. Use a light 3-4 kg (7-9 lb) line and a 1/0 hook. Rigs no. 20, 21 or 22. Very difficult to scale and most people consider it best to leave the scales intact as they can easily be removed with the skin when cooked.

PERCH, PEARL

Glaucosoma scapulare
Also known as Bull-eye and Nannygai.

It is golden brown with a silver belly, and a black spot at the base of the pectoral fin. The mouth is large, as are the eyes, which are black.

Another superb fish, the Western Australian Dhu-fish is very similar. The latter has a shade more brown marble tonings and the male of the species has an elongated soft dorsal ray.

The flesh is white, of very fine texture, and the table qualities are excellent.

HABITAT AND GROWTH
It is found on offshore reefs in southern Queensland and New South Wales. Travels in large schools. Grows to about 66 cm (26 in), and achieves a weight of 3.5 kg (8 lb) but the average fish caught is about 33 cm (13 in) and 1 kg (2 lb).

FISHING
Seems to feed on the fringe of a reef where there is sand, rather than on it. It is usually caught when fishing principally for snapper, which also prefer this environment. After dark they seem to rise and school about 7 or 8 metres (23-26 ft) clear of the bottom. They readily bite on most fish baits, prawns, squid and octopus. Use a 4/0 short shanked hook on an 11 kg (24 lb) nylon line and rig no. 16.

PILCHARD

Sardinops neopilchardus

The colour of a pilchard's body is silvery-blue above and silver below, there is a row of conspicuous dark blue spots on the sides, and there is a small single dorsal fin with soft rays. The very forked caudal fin has dark tips.

115

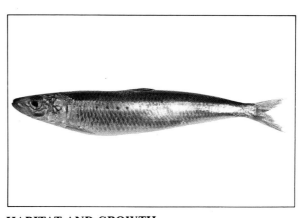

HABITAT AND GROWTH
It is very common in all states of Australia and grows to 23 cm (9 in).

FISHING
This is a very soft oily fish of the sardine family and makes excellent bait. It is netted commercially at sea but easily caught by handline and a small no. 8 hook using any prawn or piece of fish as a bait.

POMFRET, BLACK
Parastromateus niger

Also known as Black Batfish, Butterfish, Turbot and Blue Skate.

A deep-bodied, strongly compressed fish with a single continuous

dorsal and anal fin giving it a diamond-shape like that of a sweep or batfish. The blue-grey shadings of the body change from time to time, especially after death.

The flesh is firm and white and very good eating.

HABITAT AND GROWTH
Common in the tropical north half of Australia in harbours and estuaries. The black pomfret grows to 60 cm (24 in). It is always found in large schools.

FISHING
This fish seems to shoal in selective sizes and you have to fish accordingly. Use a 1/0 hook and 6 kg (14 lb) line for small fish but a 2/0 hook and a 10 kg (24 lb) line for larger fish. They are not fussy eaters and will rise to floating bait of prawn and most fish baits. Fish without a sinker if the current allows the bait to sink.

PONYFISH, BLACK-TIPPED
Leiognathus splendens
Also known as Slipmouth.

A light silvery colour with grey-green tonings above the lateral line. It is capable of projecting its mouth foward, giving it a look of a horse's head from which it derives its name. It grunts rather loudly on capture.

The common pony fish is edible.

HABITAT AND GROWTH
Common pony fish is found in coastal waters in northern New South Wales and north all along the Queensland coast. It grows to 25 cm (10 in).

FISHING
It is caught when fishing for other species. A smaller member of the family, the black-banded pony fish, is meshed in numbers by prawn trawlers. It grows to a length of only 9 cm (3½ in) and is considered trash fish.

ROSY JOB-FISH
Aprion microlepis
Also known as King Snapper, or King Emperor.

An elliptical, compressed body, with an arched dorsal profile and a prominent lower jaw. It's a handsome fish, with a glowing pale pink body and silver-white belly. The base of each scale on the

117

back and sides is bluish with a golden margin. The upper part of the head is deep pink.

The rosy job-fish is a good-quality table fish.

HABITAT AND GROWTH
Inhabits the southern Queensland reefs in much the same territory as snapper, and is often found with a shoal of that species. That fact, plus its colour, have given rise to a tale that the 'king snapper' leads every school of true snapper. The rosy job-fish grows to about 1 m.

FISHING
Often taken by line fishermen chasing snapper on the reefs. Usually taken on a drift, and puts up a hard fight on heavy handline. Use a size 4/0 hook and a 23 kg (50 lb) line. Rig no. 16.

SALMON, ATLANTIC
Salmo salar

It has been introduced to New South Wales and New Zealand in selected dams, lakes and streams but with limited success. It is similar in shape to our trout but more silvery and a little more rounded.

Good eating.

HABITAT AND GROWTH
The Atlantic salmon's natural habitat is the North Atlantic, Canada, Russia and Greenland, where fish up to 45 kg (100 lb) have been caught. The average run of fish caught there is around 8 kg (18 lb).

FISHING
It is a prized sportfish and most are caught with a fly or spinner from the shore, or trolling from a boat at speeds of about 6 to 7 knots. Use rigs no. 4, 7, 20 or 22. The Super Duper, Flopy and Wonder Wobbler are recommended.

SALMON, AUSTRALIAN
Arripis trutta

This highly popular sportfish with beach anglers is steel blue above the lateral line and silver below. The Australian salmon is a great fighter and provides good sport for all forms of angling. It travels in huge shoals along beaches where with a surf rod, casting reel and 7 kg (15 lb) line, you can enjoy fine sport. Smaller fish enter the bays and estuaries. Not as plentiful on the New South Wales coast as they were, because of heavy netting for the canning industry.

Not good eating, as the fish is strongly flavoured and stringy.

HABITAT AND GROWTH
During January, great schools of salmon gather along the Victorian and New South Wales coast for migration to Western Australia. Further to the east, schools begin their migration along the east coast. They spawn at sea and then, as they move along the coast, they enter the bays and estuaries feeding on small baitfish such as hardyheads, pilchards and whitebait. Young fish are often known as salmon trout. The general run of fish is 1 kg (2 lb) but farther south 3-4 kg (6-9 lb) are common.

FISHING
For the smaller fish a 2/0 hook will suffice, but a 4/0 hook is needed for the larger fish. They love whitebait, but if they're not fresh they're difficult to keep on the hook when casting. One solution is to push the hook through the eyes of 4 or 5 whitebait. Pilchards are popular in the west and usually cast on ganged hooks. Don't be disappointed if you can't get whitebait or pilchards, as salmon will take most fish baits when they are in a feeding frenzy. Use a silver lure if spinning. Rigs no. 4, 6, 7, 18 or 20 are suitable.

119

SERGEANT BAKER
Aulopus purpurissatus

A round-bodied fish basically red, with a creamy-white underneath. The scales are edged with red. The flesh is white and fair tasting but it has little if any appeal to the keen fisherman because of its bones.

HABITAT AND GROWTH
Distributed in the offshore waters of southern Queensland, New South Wales, Victoria, Tasmania, South Australia and the southern coast of Western Australia. A 56 cm (22 in) fish is considered large.

FISHING
Usually caught when snapper fishing. It will take the same bait as a snapper, such as mullet fillets, prawns, squid, piece of yellowtail and tailor.

SILVER BIDDY, OVATE
Gerres ovatus
Also known as Roach. It is often referred to as a

Herring or Silverbelly and confused with a small Bream and Tarwhine.

A bright silvery fish with light mauve toning and scales which are easily displaced. The jaws are weak and can be protruded.

Too small to eat.

HABITAT AND GROWTH

Found in shallow inshore waters near the mouths of estuaries in schools, where they are taken in nets by prawn trawlers.

Common along the New South Wales coast north of Sydney and in southern Queensland, where they grow to 23 cm (9 in). Fish 15 cm (6 in) are more common.

FISHING

Usually taken by children fishing the wharves and jetties near estuary mouths using a light 3 kg (7 lb) line with a tiny no. 10 hook and prawn or fish bait.

Used as bait for snapper, flathead, emperor, mulloway and most fish. If used as live bait on a heavy line at place of capture can often give the prize for the best and biggest fish. For this exercise use a 13 kg (30 lb) line, a 6/0 hook and rig no. 15. Use a wire trace if flathead are about.

SNAPPER

Chrysophrys auratus

Snapper have a number of different legal names which are termed according to age, size and locality. On the east coast of Australia, young snapper measuring between 10 and 12 cm (4 and 4¾ in) are known as cockneys until they weigh about 700 g (25 oz), when they are called red bream. Up to about 1.5 kg (3⅓ lb) they are called squire and when they are larger than that they are known as snapper. Adult snapper have iridescent pink scales with blue spots. As they grow older the fish develop a prominent bump on top of the head and a bulge on the snout.

A universally popular eating fish.

HABITAT AND GROWTH

Snapper are found in waters off all Australian States, as well as Lord Howe Island, Norfolk Island and New Zealand. Cockneys and red bream are usually found in estuaries. Squire and snapper generally are found offshore, but they also migrate seasonally to inshore waters. Adult snapper are carnivorous and are most abundant over rocky reefs where they feed on shell beds from the sea floor. They are essentially bottom-dwelling fish and are found to the edge of the Continental Shelf to a depth of 200 m (650 ft). They can grow to 125 cm (49 in) and weigh as much as 20 kg (44 lb). The average size of the fish taken is between 2 and 2.5 kg (4 to 6 lb). They spawn in spring and early summer in moderately sheltered waters in and around the estuary mouth and protected bays. The eggs are externally fertilised and hatch in a few days. They are sexually mature in 5 years.

Adult

Juvenile

FISHING
Best baits are pilchards, prawns, bonito, yellowtail, mullet, mackerel, squid and octopus. Hooks according to size of fish likely to be encountered; size 4/0 is a good start. Use rig no. 16.

SPINEFOOT, BLACK
Siganus fuscescens
Also known as Black Trevally, Blue Spotted Trevally, Mi Mi and Stinging Bream.

It is capable of rapid colour changes. On capture dark spots appear and then vanish and reappear again all in a matter of seconds. Basically olive in colour with dark blotches and tiny light blue spots all over. The fins are spiny and are capable of inflicting a painful wound.

The flesh is white and fairly coarse and good eating.

HABITAT AND GROWTH
They are often seen in large schools in shallow coral waters and in weed patches in rivers and estuaries in the tropical north. It grows to about 35 cm (14 in).

FISHING
They have a small mouth and a 1/0 hook is ample with a 7 kg (15 lb) line. They are not usually fished for but are often caught when fishing for other species with a small hook. Handle with care and avoid the spiny fins.

STRIPEY
Lutjanus carponotatus

It varies in colour from red to golden brown, flushed with pink and carries ten or more narrow brownish yellow bands along the

entire length of the fish lengthwise. The fins are yellow with sometimes a tinge of orange.

The flesh is white and firm and good eating.

HABITAT AND GROWTH
It attains a length of 38 cm (15 in) and is found on the coral reefs of North Queensland and along the top end of Australia. It is occasionally caught further south to Moreton Bay.

FISHING
It is usually caught when fishing for other reef fish. It will readily take any fresh bait, prawn or crab. Use a 3.0 or 4.0 hook on a 9 kg (20 lb) line.

TARWHINE
Rhabdosargus sarba
Also known as Silver Bream.

Closely related to the bream family, but distinguished by its silver colouring, yellow fins and more rounded head.

Tarwhine makes good eating.

HABITAT AND GROWTH
It occurs over a good portion of Australia, from southern Queensland to the Gippsland Lakes in Victoria, and from Albany to Shark Bay in Western Australia. It is not found on the southern or northern coasts. Often found in areas frequented by bream. It grows to about 1.5 kg (3 lb) although those caught are usually about 500 g (1 lb).

FISHING
Generally caught when fishing for bream. Use the same gear and

bait. A light 3 kg (6 lb) nylon line, a 1/0 short shanked hook and rig no. 3 or 13. In strong current use rig no. 21. Best baits are prawns, pipis, mullet and pilchard.

TRUMPETER
Pelates quadrilineatus
Also known as Four-lined Grunter

The trumpeter is golden with a greenish tint, a series of five or six dark brown stripes running the entire length of the body and silvery on the belly. It has a habit of emitting a series of rapid grunts when hauled free of the water.

HABITAT AND GROWTH
Very common in estuaries and harbours, especially around wharves and jetties. Trumpeter range around the entire coastline, but grow only to a length of 20 cm (8 in).

FISHING
Children find great pleasure in catching trumpeter. Use a light 3 kg (6 lb) nylon line and a no. 8 hook with a tiny split shot and rig no. 13.

TRUMPETER, BANDED

Terapon theraps
Also known as Spikey Trumpeter and Northern Grunter.

Basically olive-brown and silver with darker bands running the length of the fish incuding the caudal (tail) fin. These dark bands

125

are also evident on all the other fins.

The flesh is white and of reasonable texture and quite good eating but it is mostly cut up for bait.

HABITAT AND GROWTH
It frequents bays and estuaries all along the top end of Australia from Moreton Bay upwards where it attains a length of about 24 cm (9½ in).

FISHING
It is often taken for bait in a net or with a light 3 kg (6 lb) line and a small no. 1 hook using prawn or any fish bait. Use rig no. 31.

WHITING, SAND OR SILVER
Sillago ciliata

Greenish brown with golden reflections and a white belly. The body is elongated, has scales, 2 dorsal fins with spots and a forked tail. The anal fin is soft, as is the second dorsal which is the same length.

Excellent table fish, as the flesh is white and firm and good eating.

HABITAT AND GROWTH
Found in shallow water over sand flats and in small sand channels at the mouth of rivers right along the east coast and the southern coast. It grows to a length of 46 cm (18 in) but most fish caught are about 33 cm (13 in).

FISHING
Use a 4 kg (10 lb) line with a no. 3 to 4 hook with a light running sinker and a trace about 46 cm (18 in) long. Use rig no. 21. Best baits are beach worms, pipis, mussels and prawns.

WHITING, SCHOOL
Sillago bassensis

The elongated body is rusty brown above and silvery white below, but the colour intensity varies with the locality. At times the fish may be almost translucent.

The flesh is white and palatable and good eating.

HABITAT AND GROWTH

School whiting usually occur in inshore waters near the surf zone along the temperate coasts. It can grow to 20 or 30 cm (8 or 12 in) and weigh up to 300 g (10½ oz).

FISHING

Use rig no. 4, a light 3.5 kg (8 lb) nylon line and a no. 4 hook. It will take a small peeled prawn, pipi or mussel, but worm is by far the best bait. A slow moving bait is ideal.

WHITING, SPOTTED OR KING GEORGE

Sillaginodes punctatus

It has an elongated, rounded body, the upper half of which varies in colour from light to dark brown and is covered in dark brown spots. The lower half of the body is silvery and the comidal fin is

yellow grey. The fish have a silver or golden pink skin depending on the locality.

King George or spotted whiting is considered by many to be one of the finest table fish in Australia.

HABITAT AND GROWTH

Ranges along the temperate southern coasts and around Tasmania. It can grow to 70 cm (27 in) and more than 4 kg (10 lb) but specimens larger than 50 cm (20 in) are rare. Most fish caught weigh from 250 to 500 g (½ to 1 lb). The smaller fish usually inhabit the shallow waters of inlets and estuaries and move to the ocean beaches when they grow larger. Females mature at 4 years and spawning occurs in May and June.

FISHING

Fishing is best on sandy coastal beaches or in sandy spits near the coast. Use a 4 kg (8 lb to 10 lb) nylon line with a no. 3 or no. 4 shanked hook and rig. no. 21. Best bait is beach worms, pipi, peeled fresh green prawn or a squid leg.

WHITING, TRUMPETER

Sillago maculata

Also known as Winter Whiting.

The body is elongate and generally silvery in colour with golden-brown blotches and a lighter longitudinal band on its sides. A dark spot at the base of the pectoral fin is a distinguishing mark. The dorsal is long and in two parts, the first having 10 or 11 spines.

The flesh is white, of fine texture and flavour.

HABITAT AND GROWTH

Found in large schools in shallow coastal waters on sandy muddy bottoms and near weedy patches along the coast of NSW, Queensland, Victoria and Western Australia where it attains a size of 36 cm (14 in) and about 700 g (1½ lb). Juveniles live close inshore on worms and small crustaceans but move to deeper water as they reach maturity. During winter they move closer inshore.

FISHING

Move in huge schools close inshore in winter and provide great sport and enjoyment to anglers. Catches of 50 or more are quite common on a single outing. The average fish taken is about 23 cm (9 in). Best bait is sandworm or bloodworm but it will take a piece of peeled prawn, pipi or a small strip of fresh squid. Use a light 4 kg (9 lb) line, no. 6 hook and rig no. 21.

CHAPTER SEVEN

Fish with a Deep Fork

AMBERJACK
Seriola dumerili

A close relative of, and very often confused with, the yellowtail kingfish. Body is elongate with a deeply forked tail. Only the colouring is different, with a slight fin variation. The dorsal and ventral fins are slightly longer than those of the kingfish, and darkish blue; the wide lateral band is bright yellow. It is purple-brown on the upper body and creamy-white underneath.

Large fish are coarse, but a small fish, bled at capture, is a presentable food.

HABITAT AND GROWTH
The amberjack is common in the mid-coastal waters of our continent. It is taken at all depths on or near reefs. It attains a weight of 36 kg (80 lb), but fish about 5 kg (11 lb) are common.

FISHING
Caught in commercial quantities, generally by using a feather lure with a 6/0-8/0 hook on a 23 kg (50 lb) line behind a boat travelling at about 6 knots. However, for good sport, use a 9 kg (20 lb) line and rig no. 1, 5 or 6.

BARRACOUTA

Thysites atun

Body elongate and compressed. Steely blue on the back and lighter on the sides and undersides. Large mouth with three enlarged teeth on upper jaw. Small scales are easily shed. After spawning in summer, it is in very poor condition, so is referred to as an 'axe handle'. In this condition barracouta are sometimes infested with cestode worms and take on a milky look.

Otherwise, a food fish of good edible quality.

HABITAT AND GROWTH
Barracouta prefers the colder waters of Victoria, Tasmania, South Australia and Western Australia and the southern half of New South Wales. It grows to 1.37 m (54 in) long and weighs up to 4.5 kg (10 lb); average weight is 1.5-2 kg (3-4 lb).

FISHING
Barracouta take artificial lures freely and most are caught with feather lures from boats travelling at about 5 knots. It has

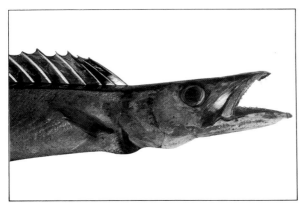

vicious teeth and care must be taken when removing the hook.
Use a 9 kg (20 lb) nylon line, wire trace, a 6/0 hook and rig no. 1
or 5.

BARRACUDA, STRIPED

Sphyraena lewini
Also known as Long-Finned Pike.

The body of the striped barracuda is elongate and compressed. It
has small scales and is steel blue on the back with silver tonings
on the sides and underside. The large mouth has an impressive
array of teeth and care must be taken when handling.
   This is not a good eating fish. The flesh is coarse and
flavourless and becomes soft soon after death.

HABITAT AND GROWTH
This fish ranges the entire southern coastline of Australia from
New South Wales to Western Australia including Tasmania. It
inhabits close offshore areas, bays and estuaries, never venturing
too far from the open sea. It grows to 51 cm (20 in).

FISHING
Barracuda take artificial lures freely and the feather lure is
popular. The boat should be travelling about 5 knots. Use a 10 kg
(22 lb) line and a 6/0 hook with wire trace and rig no. 1 or 5.

131

BREAM, BONY
Nematalosa erebi
Also known as Hair Back Herring

The bony bream is a silvery-gold all over, including the fins. The dorsal fin is greatly elongated at the base compared with other species of bream.

The flesh is white and palatable, but the fish are bony, as the name implies.

HABITAT AND GROWTH
This fresh and saltwater species is found in Victoria, South Australia, New South Wales, Queensland and the Northern Territory. It grows to 40 cm (16 in) and weighs up to 750 g (1⅔ lb). Spawning occurs in spring, in fresh or brackish water above the tidal influence.

FISHING
Not usually sought. It has a very light bite and is a great bait stealer. Use a 1/0 hook and a 2.2 kg (5 lb) line and rig no. 2 or 21. Usually caught in fresh or brackish water.

COWANYOUNG
Trachurus declivis
Also known as Horse Mackerel, Jack Mackerel and Scad.

Often confused with yellowtail, a renowned baitfish. The colouring is similar, yellowish-green above the lateral line and silver below. The lateral line of the body is armed with 74 or more broad-keeled scutes (the yellowtail has 73 scutes). The body of the scad is slightly more robust.

An excellent baitfish.

HABITAT AND GROWTH
It is generally found in offshore waters and will attain a length of 46 cm (18 in) although the general run of fish is about half that size.

FISHING
Caught only for bait. Use a very small no. 10 blackfish hook, a small piece of prawn, light nylon line and rig no. 21.

DART
Trachinotus russelli
Also known as Swallowtail.

Body moderately slender, compressed, with a deeply forked caudal fin. It is blue-grey on the upper body and silver below with five or six blotches midway just above the lateral line.
 It is good eating.

HABITAT AND GROWTH
This fine little fighting fish is most often caught in the surf from the mid-coast of New South Wales as far north as Cape York. Dart grows to about 60 cm (24 in) but the average caught is about 25-30 cm (10-12 in).

FISHING
Fish light with a 3½ kg (8 lb) line, no. 2 longshank hook baited with worm, pipi or prawn and rig no. 3. The dart will take most fish baits and will strike at a line. Use rig no. 7.

DIAMOND FISH, SILVER

Monodactylus argenteus
Also known as Butterfish and Butter Bream.

Body deep, narrow and squat. It is bright silver with a greenish tint on the back. Two vertical dark bands at the head and gills of the juvenile fish fade as the fish matures. The caudal fin is tinted yellow, as is the trailing edge of all the fins. The leading tips of the dorsal and anal fins are smudged in black.

Larger specimens are most acceptable table fish.

HABITAT AND GROWTH
Plentiful in bays and estuaries around wharves and jetties all along the coast. Grows to a length of 27 cm (10½ in).

FISHING
Diamond fish are caught with a floating bait of squid, octopus or fish, using a very small no. 7 or 8 hook on 2 kg (4½ lb) line. A luderick rig is ideal. Prawn is good acceptable bait, but it is soft and too easily stolen by smaller fish.

DOLPHIN FISH

Coryphaena hippurus

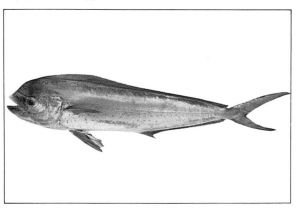

Sportfishing organisations are moving to change the name to 'mahi mahi' or 'dorado' to avoid confusion with the dolphin. A beautifully coloured fish whose body colours change when landed. The head is olive green, the body is an iridescent green-blue with numerous spots, merging to a golden belly. The colours fade and then become brilliant again. On death, they vanish and the fish becomes a dull grey.

The flesh is white and firm and very good eating.

HABITAT AND GROWTH

Dolphin fish are found in many oceans but prefer tropical waters. Occasionally they venture as far south as Sydney latitudes on both coasts. For that to happen the water temperature must be 21°C (70°F) or more. They grow to about 36 kg (80 lb), but fish around 1·5 kg (2-11 lb) are commonly caught. Dolphin fish are more likely to be found wherever there is debris in the ocean. Small baitfish use the packing cases and flotsam for a home, thus attracting the dolphin fish.

FISHING

An offshore surface fish which prefers small garfish, mullet and yellowtail, dolphin fish nevertheless readily take a lure trolled at around six knots. There seems to be no preference in lures, but the coloured feather is probably the most successful, simply because it's the most commonly used. Once hooked, dolphin fish fight hard, dashing about wildly and making spectacular leaps. Use 12 to 15 kg (26-34 lb) line, a 5/0 to 8/0 hook, a wire trace and rigs no. 5, 6 or 17.

FLUTE-MOUTH, DEEP SEA

Fistularia petimba

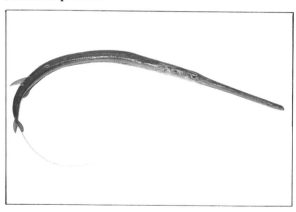

A greatly elongate fish with a body that is broader than deep and a slender tube-like snout terminating in a narrow mouth. The middle ray of the caudal fin projects as a long filament.

The flesh is edible but is a small yield for such a long fish.

HABITAT AND GROWTH

They can be found in all depths on the Continental Shelf. They mostly feed on small fishes just below the surface. They are known to grow to 137 cm (54 in).

FISHING

Usually caught when trawling offshore for prawns and fishes, deep sea flute-mouth are not especially sought after.

GARFISH, RIVER
Hyporhamphus ardelio

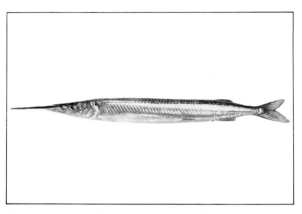

This species is similar in colouring, but lighter than the sea garfish; it is stouter, has a harder texture and larger scales.

Catching garfish is a lot of fun and as a table fish it is very good.

HABITAT AND GROWTH
It inhabits shallow weedy flats and grows to a length of 35 cm (14 in).

FISHING
The river garfish can be caught all year round but bites best early in the morning when the waters are unruffled by the wind. Use a 2 kg (4 lb) line, no. 10 hook baited with dough, pieces of prawn or sand worms.

A light 2 kg (4 lb) line on a small reel mounted on a 2 m light rod is a good starter. Use a small light quill float depending on the depth at which the fish are feeding, attached to a light 1.5 kg (3 lb) cast with two or three no. 10 hooks at various depths. Attach a small split shot to the cast just above the bottom hook to avoid a tangle when casting. Garfish seem to be attracted to a red float. Cast about 5 m (15 ft) out from the boat. River garfish have a small mouth so use only a small bait. A piece of prawn, worm or most fish bait will be taken. Use a berley mix of bread, pollard and bran to entice them but don't overfeed them.

GARFISH, SEA
Hyporhampus australis
Also known as Beakie.

Sea garfish is dark green on the upper body with three narrow dark brown streaks and silvery belly. The lower jaw has a long spear-like projection.

A baitfish rather than an eating fish.

HABITAT AND GROWTH
Sea garfish, as the name implies, is an ocean species found off all coasts including Tasmania. On occasions it enters the estuaries and river mouths but it will not travel far from the entrance. It feeds in quiet shallow waters where the sun shines on sea grass

beds on which the fish feed. It grows to a length of about 45 cm (18 in) but the average caught is 33 cm (13 in). Spawning begins in October and continues throughout summer.

FISHING
Use a 3-4 kg (6-8 lb) line with a no. 10 hook baited with dough or small pieces of prawn or sand worm and rig no. 23 or 29. Berley with breadcrumbs, pollard or fat.

GARFISH, SOUTHERN SEA
Hyporhamphus melanochir
Also known as South Australian Garfish.

Very similar in shape to other species of garfish mentioned, but colouring is lighter. The body is pale green above and silvery below with a silver band running the full length of the fish. The lower jaw is extended to a spear-like projection.
    Southern sea garfish is good to eat.

HABITAT AND GROWTH
It is found in huge schools near beaches in Tasmania, Victoria, South Australia and southern shores of Western Australia. It can attain a length of 25cm (10 in). Spawning takes place in summer.

FISHING

Big quantities are taken in seine nets by professionals near sea grass in shallow water, but they are lots of fun to catch by line. Use a 2 kg (4½ lb) line and no. 10 hooks and rig as you would for river garfish.

GARFISH, SOUTHERN SNUB-NOSED

Arrhamphus sclerolepis kreffti

Also known as No-Beak Garfish, Snubbie and Short-bill.

This garfish is green with a silver underside. Three fine dark lines run the length of the fish. Unlike other types of garfish it is recognisable by the absence of the spear-like projection on the lower jaws.

White flesh of excellent table quality.

HABITAT AND GROWTH

Found along the New South Wales coast and as far north as Rockhampton, Queensland, this fish enters bays and estuaries and grows to 38 cm (15 in).

FISHING

Use a small float and let the bait hang down about 21 cm (8 in). The float can lie horizontally. Use a 3 kg (7 lb) line and a tiny hook baited with a small piece of dough, bread or bacon fat. Berley with bread, and fish the weed beds at high tide early in the morning and where there is little wind.

GEMFISH

Rexea solandri

Also known as Hake.

The gemfish is a member of the family *Gempylidae,* which includes the snoek or barracouta. This species, though known to be fairly plentiful off the New South Wales and Victorian coasts, was not exploited commercially until 1973, when New South Wales trawlers took almost one thousand tonnes of 'hake' as it had been known, in a few months. In that year the name was changed to gemfish, as it was being confused with imported

hake, a different species, and with shark fillets marketed as 'flake'.

Gemfish is a delicious fish with a delicate flavour and the thick white fillets are extremely tasty grilled, baked, smoked or fried. It has big bones which can be removed easily before eating.

HABITAT AND GROWTH
They are bottom-dwellers which live well off New South Wales, Victoria, South Australia and Tasmania.

FISHING
The fish are caught by trawlers which drag the bottom with otter trawl nets. June to September is the best period, with tonnes of gemfish being landed each day.

GOATFISH, BLACK-SPOT
Parupeneus porphyreus

A basically pink fish, including the fins, with a conspicuous black spot on the tail base immediately behind the dorsal fin. Two fleshy barbels are attached to the lower jaw, similar to the catfish.

The flesh is white and firm, and very good eating.

139

HABITAT AND GROWTH
These fish are found on sandy bottoms near close inshore reefs in New South Wales and Queensland. They could possibly range further. They grow to about 38 cm (15 in).

FISHING
A fish that is usually caught when fishing for other species, but a prize when you catch one. Use a 2/0 hook, a 7 kg (15 lb) line and rig no. 2 or 21. It is bottom feeding and uses the barbels to search out food. It will take prawn, squid and any recognised fish bait.

GOATFISH, MOTTLED
Upeneus tragula

The goatfish is something like the shape of a whiting but more robust and with two long barbels attached to the lower jaw. Some goatfish are red, others yellow, but this one has a red belly and the rest of the body, including head and fins, is dark with brown tonings. The caudal fin is forked.
   The flesh is very palatable.

HABITAT AND GROWTH
This fish is fairly common in the tropical north of Australia and found on sandy patches close to shore, where it is known to grow to 36 cm (14 in).

FISHING
A bottom feeding fish, the mottled goatfish prefers prawn and worms to fish bait. Use a 2/0 hook on a 7 kg (15 lb) line and rig no. 2 or 21.

GRINNER, LARGE-SCALED
Saurida undosquamis
Also known as Large-scaled Saury.

This species is brown-grey above the lateral line and silvery below. It is a long round-bodied fish with a rather large mouth and a series of small sharp teeth. It has a row of dark blotches along the lateral lines.
   The flesh is firm and white but has many small bones.

HABITAT AND GROWTH
Large-scaled grinner ranges through Queensland coastal waters

and the north of Australia. Maximum size is about 58 cm (23 in), but a fish 40 cm (16 in) is more usual.

FISHING
It is a bottom-feeder which will take almost any fish bait. A small grinner is top bait for Spanish mackerel and marlin, as it will troll easily without breaking up. Use an 11 kg (24 lb) nylon line, a 4/0 hook and rig no.9.

GURNARD, FLYING

Pterygotrigla picta

Also known as Latchet and Sharp-beaked Gurnard.

It has large pectoral fins that give the false impression it can fly. The fins are predominantly olive green with a large white-edged dark blue spot. The predominant colour of the body is red with green and blue spots and splashes all over The head is large and bony with two sharp projections above the mouth. A close relative the red gurnard, lacks these projections.

The flesh is firm and white and good eating.

HABITAT AND GROWTH
Flying gurnard is plentiful around Australia on the Continental Shelf where it grows to 51 cm (20 in). The average fish caught is

141

around 28 cm (11 in). It is a bottom dweller.

FISHING
Flying gurnard is caught out wide when fishing for other species such as flathead on sand and mud bottoms.

GURNARD, SHARP-BEAKED

Pterygotrigla polyommata
Also known as Latchet.

The head is completely encased in a bony armour with two strong spines protruding on the upper lip. The colour of the body is reddish above and silvery below, with two large pectoral fins. These are beautifully coloured; olive-green on the inside surface with a distinct dark blue blotch on each with white edging. The body is covered in tiny scales. The three lower rays of the pectoral fin are detached and finger-like.

The flesh is firm and white and good eating.

HABITAT AND GROWTH
Common in our offshore waters at all depths on the Continental Shelf on sand and mud bottoms. This fish ranges from about Bundaberg in Queensland, south along the southern coast to and including Western Australia and also Tasmania, where it attains a length of 50 cm (20 in).

FISHING
This fish is usually caught by handline fishermen when fishing for flathead. It is not especially fished for but often taken in the eastern States. It will readily take most fish baits, prawn and squid. Use a 3/0 hook and rig no. 2 or 21.

HERRING, GIANT

Elops australis

It is a bright silver on the sides and belly shading to an olive on the back. The fins are yellow. Only fair for eating.

HABITAT AND GROWTH
This, the largest of the herring family, grows to 122 cm (48 in) and a weight of 11 kg (25 lb). It inhabits the rivers and creeks of the northern tropical regions.

FISHING

Giant herring prefers a live bait on a light line about 9 kg (20 lb).
It will readily take a silver lure or an A.B.U. Killer trolled at
about 4 knots. Great sport but very bony.

HERRING, SPOTTED

Harengula koningsbergeri

The spotted herring is grey-green above and silvery below with a
row of dark spots from gill to tail, and a dark blotch just behind
the gills. It has a single soft dorsal and a deeply forked caudal fin.

HABITAT AND GROWTH

It is very common in Queensland and in the north of Australia
where it can often be observed in large shoals. It grows to 18 cm
(7 in).

FISHING

A very popular bait fish, it is usually caught for this purpose.

JACKASS FISH
Nemadactylus macropterus

The body is light blue above and silver below, with a broad black band across the nape in front of the dorsal ray. Juveniles have four faint bands on the body. The eye is large, the mouth small. The dorsal is convex in the middle. Good to eat.

HABITAT AND GROWTH
It is a deep water specie roaming the waters of the bottom half of Australia and Tasmania, where it grows to a length of 61 cm (24 in).

FISHING
The jackass fish is usually taken by trawlers but will readily take a fish bait, squid or prawn. Use a 2/0 hook and rig no. 16.

KINGFISH, YELLOWTAIL
Seriola lalandi

The yellowtail kingfish is an attractive streamlined fish which is purple-blue above the lateral line to the snout, with a greenish lateral band separating the silver undersides. The tail is yellow, as the name implies.

The flesh is rather dry and tasteless but palatable.

HABITAT AND GROWTH
This fine sporting fish is found around offshore reefs and estuary mouths from central Queensland, south and around to Western Australia at about the same latitude. Also found in bays and rivers and can often be seen around wharves and jetties. It grows to 60 kg (132 lb) but the general run of fish is from 2 to 8 kg (4 to 18 lb). Generally considered a surface fish, sometimes yellowtail kingfish are caught at depths of 40 fathoms (73 m) by handline fishermen.

FISHING
They are usually berleyed to the surface and caught by casting a baited hook into the school. Gear depends on the size of the fish, but usually a 14 kg (30 lb) line and 6/0 hook without lead will suffice. They will readily rise to a lure trolled at about 5 knots. Use rig no. 15, 17 or 27.

MACKEREL, QUEENSLAND SCHOOL
Scomberomorus queenslandicus

Also known as Doggie Mackerel, Blotched Mackerel and Shiny Mackerel.

The body is compressed and elongate with minute scales. It is blue-green above a rather distinct lateral line and silvery below, with a number of grey blotches along the sides. The membrane of the dorsal fin is black.

The flesh of this mackerel is superb.

HABITAT AND GROWTH
This mackerel can be found all along the Queensland coast and in mid-winter they move into bays and estuaries where they are taken in numbers by both professional and amateur fishermen. They grow to a weight of 8 kg (17 lb) but the average run of fish is about 2 kg (4 lb).

FISHING
They will readily take a silver spoon lure trolled about seven knots. A running barrel sinker of sufficient weight is necessary to keep the spoon from skipping on the surface. The sinker on the main line stopped by a single swivel about 2 m from the spoon.

145

Jig the line by hand to vary the speed. They will also take a bait on a handline, cast well out from the boat without a sinker.

MACKEREL, SLIMY
Scomber australasicus

Body elongate, soft and slippery to handle and has small scales. It is bright green with numerous green wavy blotches all over and silver tonings underneath.

A soft fish, and although many are eaten they cannot be considered a good eating fish.

HABITAT AND GROWTH
A common species found below the Capricorn line all along the coast from east to west where it attains a length of 37 cm (15 in). Travels in large schools and enters the harbours and bays usually in summer. There they are often caught in thousands by handliners. The slimy mackerel travels far upstream, preferring clear salt water. Average fish is 23 cm (9 in).

FISHING
Excellent bait and most fish, especially mulloway, find them irresistible. When schools of slimies are evident, predators such as mulloway are never far away. Slimies have a small soft mouth and a no. 8 hook is quite big enough. A 3 kg (6 lb) line is strong enough and will give good sport. Use rig no. 31.

MACKEREL, SPANISH
Scomberomorus munroi

Above the lateral line of the body Spanish mackerel is iridescent blue-green with shades of purple and bronze. The dorsal fin is bright blue. Below the lateral line the fish is off-white with darker vertical bars. A long, streamlined fish.

The flesh is white, firm and good eating.

HABITAT AND GROWTH
This is a tropical species found along the coast of the northern half of Australia from Coffs Harbour, New South Wales, to Geraldton, Western Australia, from August to December. It is a great sporting fish, growing to around 45 kg (100 lb) and 2 m (6½ ft).

146

FISHING

They seem to run in schools of fish about the same size and when hooked will leap and fight with great agility, shaking their heads to shed the hook. Trolling at about 7 knots with garfish or a hammered spoon lure or feather lure is the most common method used to catch them. Use a good stout 23 kg (50 lb) line, an 8/0 or 10/0 hook and rig no. 1, 5, 18 or 26.

MARLIN, BLACK
Makaira indica

This magnificent fish is the undisputed prized gamefish in Australia. Its fighting qualities are legendary. It is identified by its very thick deep body which is rather rounded near the head, especially in larger fish. It has a short, thick upturned bill. The pectoral fin is always erect. Other fins can be folded and recessed into indentations to streamline the fish, reducing resistance. It is steel-blue above and white below.

The flesh is white and good eating.

HABITAT AND GROWTH

Black marlin likes the warm tropical waters and is thought to breed well beyond the Continental Shelf. Grows to about 5 m (16

147

ft) and 680 kg (1500 lb). Many of these much sought-after fish are taken by long-line fishermen from other nations.

FISHING
The first recorded marlin caught and landed on the New South Wales coast was in 1910 by Dr Mark Lidwell off Port Stephens. The first marlin caught weighing over 450 kg (1000 lb) was taken in September 1968 off Cairns, Queensland, by Bob Walker on an 80 lb breaking strain line.

When a marlin takes the baited hook it runs for many metres and anglers need great self-control to stem the urge to strike. Knowing when to strike after the fish has made the initial run and then swallowed the bait is a matter of feel. But if you have displayed control and the hook bites home, you can be assured you are in for a lively time. The marlin will play all the antics imaginable, leaning, twisting and turning and tearing through the water at a great pace.

Black marlin generally begin their fight deep down and it can be some time before they surface and take to the air. They are usually caught with a large baitfish such as bonito, yellowtail, kingfish, Australian salmon or sea mullet trolled on the surface at a speed of 4 to 6 knots. It is important that the trailed baitfish does not twist, but planes on the surface.

Plastic squid and Knucklehead are among the most popular lures. The use of a lure means striking much earlier and driving the hook into the soft part of the mouth, which is very difficult to find. Experts say the smaller fish will readily take a lure, but the big fellows will not be tricked. Lures need to be trolled at about 10 knots.

North of Cairns where the big black marlin are taken, the top fishermen use Spanish mackerel and rainbow runner rigged on a bridle.

MARLIN, BLUE
Makaira mazara

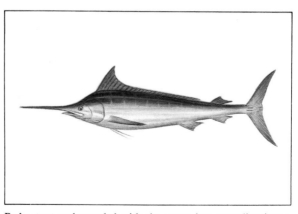

Body stout and rounded with the upper jaw extending into a spear-like projection. Blue marlin is purple-blue above, silvery below with blue vertical stripes on the upper part. The colourings are brilliant but fade quickly after capture. The pectoral fins fold flat against the body.

Blue marlin is rarely eaten.

HABITAT AND GROWTH
Range all along the east, west and northern coasts of Australia

and in fact over most of the Pacific, where they grow to a weight of up to 820 kg (1800 lb). It is recorded locally to 220 kg (485 lb).

FISHING
Caught in the same manner as are other marlin.

MARLIN, STRIPED
Tetrapturus audax

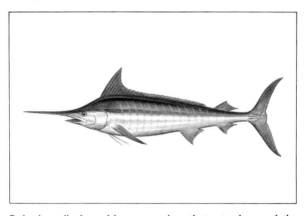

Striped marlin have 14 mauve stripes that extend around the body which is much smaller and less robust than the black marlin. The bill is long and narrow compared with the black, and the pectoral fin will fold back flat alongside the body. It is a most attractive fish with its streamlined shape and the blue colouring on the sides fading to a silvery white belly.

HABITAT AND GROWTH
There is evidence that marlin numbers have been depleted in the last decade and every year sees a further decline. The long-line fishermen from other nations fishing beyond the Continental Shelf are considered a great hazard to the stocks. There is some hope that the number of fish will build up again when the new international law extending Australian territorial waters to 322 km (200 miles) off the coast has had time to take effect. The Continental Shelf extends about 46 km (25 nautical miles) from our coast and 93 km (50 nautical miles) was considered the imaginary line inside which foreign fishing vessels could not trespass.

Little is known about the breeding habits of marlin, but their breeding grounds are believed to be just beyond the Continental Shelf. If that is so, the new 322 km (200 mile) limit should have the desired effect if the law is enforced. The flesh of the marlin is considered a delicacy in Japan and Russia, and the prize may be considered worth a poaching risk.

An average fish caught is about 91 to 136 kg (200-300 lb) although the record stands at 314.54 kg (692 lb).

FISHING
Striped marlin will readily take a lure of plastic squid, knucklehead, white or red feathers trolled at a speed of around 10 knots. The same bait and technique described for the black marlin is applicable to this species. From the moment the hook bites home a striped marlin fights like fury, making mighty leaps and doing everything possible to throw it. This is how marlin

earned their title 'the prince of gamefish'. The striped marlin will fight until completely exhausted, when it will lie alongside the boat to await its fate.

MORWONG

Nemadactylus douglasii

Also commonly known as the Jackass. In New Zealand it is called Porae.

Morwong has large eyes, a small mouth and is distinguished by a greatly elongated ray on the pectoral fin. Body is silver-blue to silver-grey on top and silvery below.

The flesh is white and firm and good eating when the black abdominal coating is cleaned away before cooking.

HABITAT AND GROWTH

It can grow to a length of 60 cm (24 in) and a weight of 4 kg (9 lb.) It is bottom dwelling and is usually found at depths of between 40 and 250 metres (130-820 ft). The morwong lives on offshore reefs off southern Queensland, New South Wales, Victoria and Tasmania. Most fish caught are about 1kg (2 lb).

FISHING

Usually caught when fishing for snapper and when hooked will fight as much as that fish. Use a snapper rig, a 9 kg (20 lb) nylon line and a 3/0 hook, and fish the bottom. Use rig no. 16.

MORWONG, RED

Cheilodactylus fuscus

Colouring is a copper-red, and it has two bony protuberances growing on the snout in front of the eyes. It is caught mainly in summer and is a bream species.

Red morwong makes good eating.

HABITAT AND GROWTH

The red morwong are fairly plentiful along southern Queensland and New South Wales coasts and inhabit the rocky reefs close to shore. They grow to about 46 cm (18 in).

FISHING

Red morwong are not especially fished for, but are caught when fishing for other species using crab or cunjevoi for bait. Spear fishermen account for more kills than the conventional line fishermen.

MULLET, RED

Upeneichthys lineatus

As the name implies, this fish is red with bright blue lines between the eyes and mouth and a black spot at the base of the tail. It has two barbels (fleshy whiskers) below the mouth.

The flesh is white and good eating.

HABITAT AND GROWTH

Found in the coastal waters around Australia and New Zealand but seems to prefer the cooler waters of South Australia, Victoria, the southern shores of Western Australia and the South Island of New Zealand. Grows to about 30 cm (12 in).

FISHING

Rarely fished for by amateur fishermen, but caught when fishing with a light line for bream. An ideal rig would be no. 2, 3 or 4,

151

using a 4 to 5 kg (9-11 lb) nylon line and a 1/0 short shanked hook. Prawn and pipi are the best baits.

PIKE

Sphyraenella obtusata

A member of the Barracuda family and sometimes referred to as Snook in the southern States, Sea Striped Pike, Barracuda or Sennit.

Greenish above, silvery below, with three dark brown bands running the length of the fish. Two of these bands are above the lateral line, the other is below. The large mouth has an impressive array of powerful teeth.

The flesh is soft but good eating.

HABITAT AND GROWTH

Pike has a wide range, stretching from southern Queensland along the New South Wales coast, Victoria, South Australia and up the Western Australian coast to latitude 26°S. Usually found at the mouth of estuaries, it grows to 56 cm (22 in) although fish of 40 cm (16 in) are average.

FISHING

Pike provides great sport with light gear and will make

spectacular leaps in its effort to get free. When 'on' it is caught in large numbers and the best bait appears to be strips from the belly section of their kind. It will bite at prawn, small fish, especially hardyheads and whitebait. Use a 2/0 hook with a 4 kg (9 lb) nylon line and rig no. 19. Use minimum lead. Cast away from the boat or jetty and allow line to sink slowly, giving an occasional short pull. When line settles on the bottom, retrieve slowly and repeat the cast. Will also take a no. 5 rig trolled at 5 knots.

QUEENFISH

Scomberoides commersonianus

Also known as Leatherskin, Giant Dart, Whitefish and Skinny Fish.

Oblong, compressed body with a jutting lower jaw, large mouth and large eyes. The silvery body has 5-7 dusky blotches above the lateral line. The skin is rough and leathery, and the scales are lance-shaped and embedded.

Good if eaten fresh, but the flesh deteriorates rapidly, becoming dry and insipid.

HABITAT AND GROWTH

A wide distribution, from northern New South Wales around the north coast to the north-west coast of Western Australia. It grows to a weight of around 14 kg (30 lb) and 1 m (40 in) although the fish commonly caught by anglers is around half that size. A school fish, it is often found in greater numbers and smaller sizes in estuaries and inlets, with large specimens being taken at sea, usually near reefs and headlands.

FISHING

A spectacular fighting fish with power, speed and courage, the queenfish leaps and tailwalks when hooked, and has sufficient body depth to grip the water against the lateral pull of a fishing line. It will readily take a fish bait, and in turn makes a good bait for mackerel and flathead.

REDFISH

Centroberyx affinis

Until recently it was known as Nannygai. Shoppers at fish markets apparently didn't like the name so it was changed to Redfish.

As the name implies, this fish is red all over, with a silver belly. It has large black eyes and the gape of the mouth is unusually wide. Spines in the gill area are very sharp and care should be taken in handling them.

The flesh is firm and white and very good eating.

HABITAT AND GROWTH

Until about 1960 it was considered our most prolific fish but commercial netting has taken its toll. It is a voracious biter which travels in great schools around the fringes of reefs where snapper are usually caught. It occurs in all southern waters from southern Queensland around Victoria, South Australia to Western Australia's mid-coast. The average run of fish is about 500 g (1 lb).

FISHING

Usually caught when snapper fishing, and often considered a nuisance in spite of its good eating quality. It is a bottom feeder but seems to rise about 8 m (26 ft) after dark. It will readily take any fish baits and prawns. Use a 3/0 hook, a 9 kg (20 lb) nylon line and rig no. 16.

RUNNER, RAINBOW

Elagatis bipinnulatus

A handsome fish with brilliant colourings of dark and light blue, green fading to yellow and silvery white below. The head and body of the fish resembles that of a kingfish, to which it is related. The tail is unusually large and deeply forked.

Reasonable eating but preferred as live bait for big game.

HABITAT AND GROWTH

Runners are travelling fish, distributed in the temperate and tropical waters off New South Wales, Queensland, the tropical north and Western Australia. Found in inshore coastal waters and near coral reefs. It grows to about 120 cm (47 in) and 9 kg (20 lb), but the average fish is around 50 cm (20 in).

FISHING

They travel in schools and are usually caught fishing deep on the outer reefs. Marlin anglers prize them as bait. Use a strong 4/0 to 6/0 hook on a 9 kg (20 lb) line and any fresh fish bait. Rig no. 9 and fish near the bottom. It will rise to a trolled bait of pilchard, garfish or mullet fillet, or a lure travelling at about 4 knots. The Christmas Tree type is recommended.

SAILFISH

Istiophorus platypterus

The general shape of the sailfish resembles that of marlin, and the colouring is a brilliant blue fading away to a silvery white below the lateral line. The magnificent sail-like dorsal fin, from which it gets its name, is spotted with blue and black.
The flesh is edible.

HABITAT AND GROWTH

Sailfish, like marlin, come to the surface at times to feast on small baitfish. However, the contents of their stomachs prove they also take a toll of bottom-dwelling fish. Caught in many parts of the world in warm tropical waters, especially around Panama. In Australia, the fishing grounds are the Torres Straits, northern Queensland and around the Great Barrier Reef. On rare occasions they have ventured as far south as Port Stephens on the mid New South Wales coast. Also found in numbers off the northern parts of Western Australia. Most of the sailfish caught in our waters are about 36 kg (80 lb). A fish over 45 kg (100 lb) is a fine catch and a fish over 56 kg (125 lb) could make the record book. The world record is 100.45 kg (221 lb).

FISHING

Most sailfish are respected for their fine fighting qualities. They are usually caught on light rod and gear, brought alongside the boat, tagged and allowed to go free. They put on a great show when hooked, leaping about and fighting with great vigour. Sailfish will readily take a lure of plastic squid, Knucklehead, and white or red feathers trolled at a speed of about 8 knots. The same baits and technique used for the black marlin apply.

SAMSON FISH
Seriola hippos

Often mistaken for a Yellowtail Kingfish and in Western Australia it is also known as Sea Kingfish.

The samson fish is blue-green above the lateral line and silver or white below. The dorsal fins are golden yellow. Its red teeth are a distinguishing feature, and as the name suggests, the samson fish is a strong swimmer.

The flesh is a little strong but good eating.

HABITAT AND GROWTH

The samson fish is found along the coast of New South Wales and southern Queensland and the south and west coasts of Western Australia. Specimens in Western Australia have been known to grow bigger than 50 kg (110 lb) but fish that size are exceptional. The average is around 5-8 kg (11-18 lb).

FISHING

Readily takes most fish baits, especially live yellowtail, hardyhead and pilchard. A good sporting fish. Use a 14 kg (30 lb) nylon line with a strong 4/0 to 6/0 hook. Use rig no. 15 with just enough lead to hold near the bottom.

SNOOK

Sphyraena novaehollandiae

Also known as Sea Pike, Short-finned Pike or Short-finned Barracuda, which it closely resembles.

It belongs to the barracuda family and has the slender characteristic body. The snook is not banded as is the pike, and is bright green above the lateral line and silver below. The tail is greenish yellow with a darker green edge. It has canine type teeth which can inflict a painful wound if handled carelessly.

The flesh is a good edible quality.

HABITAT AND GROWTH

Found in all Australian States near estuary mouths and grows to about 1 m (3 ft) and 5 kg (11 lb). Fish half that size are usual.

FISHING

Best rig is 4/0 hooks in chain with garfish or pilchard (mulie) as bait, which can be cast and retrieved. Use an 11 kg (24 lb) line and rig no. 19. Snook will readily take a lure, but the type is a matter of trial and error. Try rig no. 6. Many snook are caught trolling a silver lure, Christmas Tree and Killers behind a boat travelling at about 4 knots.

SWEEP
Scorpis lineolatus

This species is smaller than *Scorpis aequipinnis* and is a brilliant blue-black. The body is covered with small scales extending to the base of the fins.

The flesh is firm and white, is good eating, but it is only a small fish.

HABITAT AND GROWTH
Caught along the Victorian coast in good numbers. It schools close offshore and around wharves close to the open sea. Grows to about 25 cm (10 in) but fish of 18 cm (7 in) are common.

FISHING
It rises to a bait and steals it if the hook is too large. Use prawn or any fish bait, a 5 kg (11 lb) line and no. 4 hook. Use rig no. 9.

SWEEP, BANDED
Scorpis aequipinnis

There are several species of sweep but this one is brownish above and lightish below. It has a small mouth and the body shape resembles that of a bream — deep and compressed.

The flesh is firm and good eating.

HABITAT AND GROWTH
Found in Western Australia, South Australia and Tasmania, it inhabits rocky shores where it plays around and feeds in the broken water. It grows to a length of 38 cm (15 in).

FISHING
It is usually caught when fishing for snapper, when at times it is a nuisance. It has a small mouth and steals the snapper bait, particularly fish bait, prawns, cunjevoi and squid. Use a 5 kg (11 lb) nylon line, a no. 4 hook and rig no. 31.

TAILOR
Pomatomus saltatrix
Also known as Choppers and Blue-Fish

Body elongated and compressed and covered with very small scales. It is dark blue-green above, fading on the sides to silvery below. It has small sharp teeth in a rather large mouth. The tail fin is forked.

The flesh is inclined to be soft but good eating if cooked and eaten soon after being caught. Many anglers smoke their catch. The fish should be bled as soon as it is captured.

HABITAT AND GROWTH
Tailor grow to a weight of 14 kg (31 lb) but the Australian record catch is 9.63 kg (21 lb 3 oz). Tailor is mainly an ocean species but will enter the harbours and estuaries and penetrate far upstream close to brackish water. Mainly a surface fish, it feeds at all depths and is often caught at 30 fathoms. It travels up the east and west coasts with predictable regularity each year. Tailor appear around Broken Bay and Sydney Harbour as 'choppers' (small fish of about 500 g (1 lb)) and Perth, during February. By April the average weight has improved to 1 kg (2 lb). Peak period appears to be April, May and June. By September they're running hot off Fraser Island and Shark Bay. They feed on small fish such as pilchards (mulies), whitebait, yellowtail, hardyheads, small mullet and garfish. Tailor are found in all southern States, including Tasmania.

FISHING

If you fish the beach or rocks, you will need a surf rod, a casting reel and a 7 kg (15 lb) nylon line, three ganged 4/0 hooks, baited with a pilchard, garfish or a slab of pike. Large numbers of tailor are taken with a silver lure cast well out and retrieved. Boat fishermen enjoy good sport by trailing a silver lure, Christmas Tree or Killer lure at about 4 knots. If the line picks up any weed the fish will not touch it. Consequently, if fish are evident, and you are not getting a strike, check for weed. If they are shy, a variation of speed will sometimes entice a strike. They are strong fighters and you can enjoy great sport when they are on. Use rig no. 6, 7, 16 or 18.

TOMMY-RUFF

Arripis georgianus

In the west it is often referred to as a Ruff or Sea Herring.

This fish is closely related to the Australian salmon, being similar in shape and colouring, green above the lateral line and silver below.

Excellent table quality.

HABITAT AND GROWTH

Tommy-ruff occurs along the southern shores from southern NSW to the mid-coast of Western Australia. It grows to a length of only 41 cm (16 in) but travels in large schools and stays close to the mouths of estuaries and the coast.

FISHING

It provides good fast sport from a boat, beach or rock. Not a fussy eater, and will take most baits, including prawns, worms, pilchards and whitebait. Use no. 8 to 10 hook on a 7 kg (15 lb) nylon line and rig no. 21 or 31.

TREVALLY, BLUE SPOTTED

Caranx bucculentus

Also known as Wide-mouthed Trevally.

A deep-bodied fish, pale olive green above the lateral line and silvery below. The adult fish has blue spots scattered over the

upper half. All fish have a dark spot on the gill cover.
The blue spotted trevally provides good eating.

HABITAT AND GROWTH
It is common in coastal waters of the tropical north from the
Tropic of Capricorn where it attains a length of 77 cm (30 in).

FISHING
It is a strong fighter and will give good sport on a 14 kg (30 lb)
line with a strong 6/0 hook. A floating bait is best, live if possible
but any fresh fish bait or prawn will suffice. Use rig no. 7, 15 or
18.

TREVALLY, CALE CALE
Ulua mandibularis

It is olive green above and silvery below. The fins are green with
dark tonings and there are a series of faint dusky vertical bands
over the body and head. These bands become fainter with age.
The flesh is firm and good eating.

HABITAT AND GROWTH
Cale cale trevally attains a length of 66 cm (26 in) and is found in
the offshore waters of northern Queensland, the tropical north of
Western Australia and all along Australia's top end.

161

FISHING

Generally caught fishing cays on the Great Barrier Reef and coral reefs in Torres Strait and the far north. They like a small live baitfish but will readily take a cut fish bait, prawn or hermit crab. Use a 4/0 to 6/0 hook, a 14 kg (30 lb) line and just enough lead to float the bait. Rig no. 7 or 15.

TREVALLY, GREAT
Caranx sexfasciatus

Often confused with the turrum which it closely resembles in colour and shape, but distinguishable by the 19-21 rays of the dorsal fin. The turrum has 29-31 rays. The body is elongate and deep, light shades of blue above with golden tonings and silvery below. The caudal fin is strong and deeply forked. There is a black spot on the gill cover.

The flesh is firm and good eating while the fish is small, but tends to be flavourless in large fish.

HABITAT AND GROWTH

Found in large schools in shallow bays on the tropical coast where it grows to 120 cm (47 in) and 36 kg (80 lb).

FISHING

Will take most fish baits and is a great fighter. Found at all depths. Use a 4/0 or 6/0 hook on a 27 kg (60 lb) line and rig no. 4 with only a small piece of lead to allow the bait to float down.

TREVALLY, LOWLY
Caranx ignobilis

A light golden shade of fish all over including the fins. It is a deep-bodied and a beautifully proportioned fish.

The flesh is firm and good eating.

HABITAT AND GROWTH

A large species of the family attaining a weight of 23 kg (50 lb). It is found at sea near coral reefs in the northern half of Australia.

FISHING
Prefers live baitfish but will take any fresh fish bait or prawn.
Use a strong 6/0 or 8/0 hook and a rig no. 7, 15 or 18.

TREVALLY, SILVER
Caranx nobilis
Also known as White Trevally.

A clean, attractive-looking fish with green-gold on top fading to
a yellow-gold on the sides with silver underneath. The tail is
greenish and has a very deep 'v' shape. The pectoral fin is long
and green-gold.

The flesh is good eating but it does not keep as well as other
fish such as snapper and morwong.

HABITAT AND GROWTH
This trevally is the common variety found off the eastern coast
of Australia from central Queensland to Tasmania and South
Australia as well as New Zealand. The average size of fish
caught is about 50 cm (20 in) but it grows to 110 cm (43 in). It
feeds mainly on small fish on and around rocky shorelines and
reefs in schools of similar-sized fish.

163

FISHING

When hooked it puts up a fight equal to or better than most fish its size, and will take most baitfish. Use a line and hook according to the size of fish sought. A 5 kg (11 lb) line with a 2/0 hook is all right for a 500 g (1 lb) fish caught closer inshore and near the coast, but a 9 kg (20 lb) line with a 4/0 hook is required if you are fishing wide where the run of fish can be from 1 to 3 kg (2 to 7 lb). The larger fish are most often caught when fishing for snapper. Rigs can be used either from a boat in shallow water, no. 4 or 17; or from a boat in deep water offshore, no. 16; or from the rocks, no. 17.

TRUMPETER, BASTARD

Latridopsis forsteri

Also known as Striped Trumpeter.

The bastard trumpeter is a pinkish-bronze above the lateral line, silvery below, with pinkish dark-edged fins. The lips are thick.
  One of the most sought after fish in southern waters.

HABITAT AND GROWTH

The bastard trumpeter occurs in Tasmania, Victoria, N.S.W. and South Australia as well as New Zealand. It grows to a considerable size but in Tasmania, Victoria and South Australia the usual run of fish is 2-3 kg (5-6 lb). It inhabits offshore reefs at depths to 70 fathoms and preys on squid, prawns and small fish. It will readily take a bait of fresh barracuda. It growns to a length of 1.5 metres (5 ft) and a weight of 27 kg (60 lb).

FISHING

Small immature fish inhabit the bays and inlets where a 5 kg

(11 lb) breaking strain line with a 2/0 hook and enough lead to get to the bottom will suffice. According to size of fish and depths, offshore use a 14 kg (30 lb) line and a 4/0 to 6/0 hook and rig no. 9 or 16.

TUNA ALBACORE

Thunnus alalunga
Also known simply as Tuna.

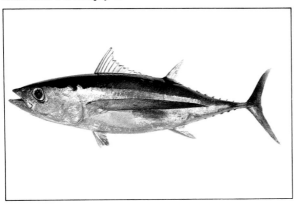

One of the tuna family; a robust fish and a very strong swimmer. The elongated and compressed body is dark green-blue above the lateral line and silver below. The edges of the tailfin and fins are yellow. Small sharp teeth. The lower half of the juveniles' bodies are marked with dark longitudinal streaks.

The flesh is not quite as meaty as most other tuna, but if blanched in boiling water for one minute, is quite presentable for grilling and frying in steaks about 1 cm (3/8 in) thick.

HABITAT AND GROWTH
Albacore is found in deep offshore waters where it is generally fished extensively by Japanese longline trawlers. Albacore preys on small baitfish such as pilchards, whitebait, cowanyoung and garfish. It attains a weight of 27 kg (60 lb) but the average fish captured is about 5 kg (11 lb).

FISHING
It will readily take a feather lure trolled about 6 knots. Use rig no. 1 to no. 5 or 6. Also good is a bobby cork with a cast about 3 m (10 ft) below, a live baitfish on an 8/0 hook and 9 kg (20 lb) nylon line rig no. 17.

TUNA BONITO

Sarda australis
Also called Tuna, Stripey or Striped Tuna.

Surface fish which is blue-green above and silvery below with a number of dark narrow bands running the entire length of the body. The fins are grey. The body is elongate and rounded. A single row of small teeth on both jaws.

The flesh of the bonito is very meaty-flavoured, and not good to eat. It makes excellent bait for snapper and other deep-sea reef dwellers.

HABITAT AND GROWTH
Bonito ranges along the entire coast of Australia feeding on small baitfish close inshore. It grows to a maximum weight of 6 kg (13 lb).

165

FISHING

Fishermen troll a lure about five knots on the way to the fishing grounds to pick up bonito for bait. Feathers, Smiths jigs, A.B.U. Killers and Christmas Trees are all good lures.

TUNA, MACKEREL

Euthynnus affinis

Also known as Little Tuna and Bonito.

One of the tuna family, with robust body tapering to a narrow peduncle. It is bright blue-black above, silvery white below, and there are usually five rounded dark blotches on the belly between the pectoral and ventral fins. The two dorsal fins are barely separated. Above the lateral line there is a series of backwardly-running oblique dusky lines. A dark-fleshed fish, it's preferred more for bait and berley than for eating.

HABITAT AND GROWTH

Schools in inshore coastal waters and reefs from about the

Murchison River in WA around the north coast and down the east to about Eden in NSW. The size usually taken is about 75 cm (30 in) although it is known to grow to about 1.2 m (4 ft)

and 13.5 kg (30 lb). Its common name stems from its liking for the same habitat as mackerel.

FISHING
Trolling is the usual method, and light game fishermen often pick up several to use as live bait, troll bait or berley on their way out to deeper water. It feeds on blue sprats, herring and pilchards, and fished live, these are a worthwhile bait. Knuckleheads and feathers on heavy handlines are the usual rigs.

TUNA, NORTHERN BLUEFIN
Thunnus tonggol

Dark blue above with silvery sides and spots in five longitudinal rows. The caudal fin is forked; the body elongate and thick.
   Its flesh is light, but a little soft.

HABITAT AND GROWTH
This fine sporting fish grows to about 23 kg (50 lb) though the average fish caught weighs about 11.4 kg (25 lb). Found in the warmer waters along the Australian coast, above Busselton in Western Australia and Eden in NSW. Northern bluefin tuna feeds on small baitfish such as yellowtail, garfish, hardyheads, pilchards and mackerel.

FISHING
Good light game fishing and readily takes a white lure trolled at about 6 knots. Use a 9 kg (20 lb) nylon line and an 8/0 strong hook and boat rod to suit. Use rigs no. 1, 5, 6 or 17 with live bait.

TUNA, SOUTHERN BLUEFIN
Thunnus maccoyii

Largest of the tuna family, growing to better than 136 kg (300 lb). Dark blue to blue-green on the back above the lateral line and silvery below. The edges of the fins are yellow. The caudal fin is forked and the body is covered with small scales.
   Although sought by the canning industry, its flesh is too meaty and strong to be eaten fresh.

HABITAT AND GROWTH

This much sought-after tuna is widely spread in the coastal waters off southern NSW, Tasmania, Victoria, South Australia and southern Western Australia. It grows to 1.8 m (6 ft) but the average taken is 13-27 kg (30-60 lb).

FISHING

Extensively fished for out of Eden on the NSW south coast for canning. It feeds on small baitfish but is usually caught with long line or feathered lures from professional tuna boats, well to seaward. Mostly taken with a feather, Christmas Tree, or Knucklehead lure at 6-7 knots by game fishermen.

TUNA, STRIPED

Katsuwonus pelamis

This Tuna is also known as Skipjack or Stripey.

The colour is brilliant deep blue above with silver below the lateral line, which is an irregular shape. All the fins are dark grey.

The flesh has a strong, meaty flavour, and is poor eating. It is an excellent baitfish for snapper and morwong and most bottom-dwelling fish on offshore reefs.

HABITAT AND GROWTH
Found in the southern half of the continent from NSW to Western Australia close inshore where it schools in great numbers. It attains a maximum weight of 6 kg (13 lb).

FISHING
It will freely take an artificial lure trolled astern of a boat travelling at about 5 knots. Use a 9 kg (20 lb) line and rig no. 1, 5 or 6, a small live baitfish such as yellowtail, pilchard, hardyhead, tailor and slimy mackerel on a 6/0 or 8/0 hook and rig no. 17. It is a surface fish.

TUNA, YELLOWFIN
Thunnus albacares

The yellowfin tuna is a dark blue above the lateral line and silvery below, with elongated spots. The fins are bright yellow and sometimes have dark tips.

As with most surface fish, the flesh is inclined to be a bit meaty. The eating qualities can be improved by cutting away the red meat and boiling the white meat for 1 minute before frying or grilling. The flesh is not especially good eating, unless canned.

HABITAT AND GROWTH
This fish is caught extensively off the coast when light game fishing. It grows upwards of 45 kg (100 lb) and feeds on pilchards, garfish, whitebait, hardyheads and small baitfish.

FISHING
It will take an artificial lure. A rod or handline using a bobby cork and a hook at a depth of 5 or 6 metres (18 ft) with a live pilchard, mackerel or yellowtail will almost certainly produce results. They are extensively fished for by Japanese long-liners for canning. Use a 14 kg (30 lb) nylon line and an 8/0 hook and rig no. 1, 5, 6 or 17 with live bait.

TURRUM
Carangoides emburyi
Also known as Albacore.

Body elongate and compressed, light shades of blue above with golden tonings and silvery below. A number of darker yellow spots form 7 vertical bars. A dark line extends from the top of the gill to the caudal fin which is deeply forked. It has small fine teeth in both jaws. The dorsal is in 2 parts, the first being short (7 spines), the second beginning about halfway along the body and extending to the tail. All fins have golden tonings.

It is often confused with the great trevally which it closely resembles, but is distinguished by the dorsal fin which has 29-31 rays, whereas the great trevally has only 19-21.

Small fish are good eating, but large ones tend to be flavourless.

HABITAT AND GROWTH
This fish prefers the warm tropical waters. It grows to 41 kg (91 lb). Small fish are found in shallow offshore waters at all depths; larger fish further seaward and close to reefs.

FISHING
A much sought-after gamefish which when hooked will do its utmost to get free. It will take a lure and a Knucklehead, Christmas tinsel, silver spoon and feather are successful trolled at about 5 knots. It isn't a fussy eater but a small live bait is first choice. Use a 13 kg (30 lb) line and a 6/0 hook with rig no. 4 as a floating bait.

WAHOO

Acanthocybium solandri
Also known as Bastard Mackerel, Jack Mackerel, Mongrel Mackerel and Pike Mackerel.

Body elongate with a long snout and a single row of sharp serrated teeth in both jaws. It has small scales, a dorsal fin uniform in height for half of its length tapering away to a dark blue short soft dorsal similar in shape to the anal fin. It is a brilliant bronze blue above and silvery below with a number of wide blue bands along the body. Wahoo are good to eat.

Wahoo, far right, are recognised game fish.

HABITAT AND GROWTH
Found in warm tropical waters but occasionally taken as far south as lat. 34° (about Sydney). Wahoo feeds on small surface fish and attains a length of nearly 2 m (6 ft) and weight of about 14 kg (30 lb).

FISHING
A recognised gamefish and with light game equipment will provide a fight to be remembered. Readily takes a floating bait of live baitfish such as yellowtail, cowanyoung, garfish or small tailor on an 8/0 hook and wire trace about 2 m (6 ft) below the surface. Use a 14 kg (30 lb) line and rig no. 17 with a swivel. It will also take a lure travelling at about 5 knots. A Knucklehead or tinsel (Christmas tree) is recommended.

WHIPTAIL
Pentapodus paradiseus

Also known as the Butterfly Bream, Rainbow, Paddy and Paradise Fish.

The whiptail takes its name from the long trailing filament of the upper lobe of the caudal fin. It is a pretty fish with many colours, generally blue-green above and fading to a cream below with a bright yellow band running the entire length of the fish at about the middle. The fins are yellow and at the base of the dorsal fin on the back is a bright blue narrow band. The snout is bright blue with two yellow stripes.

The flesh is firm and white and the adult fish is well worth keeping to eat.

HABITAT AND GROWTH
It ranges the entire Queensland coast and is found over sand bottom in rivers and estuaries and close offshore where it attains a length of 33 cm (13 in).

FISHING
The whiptail is sought after as a baitfish for larger fish. They are caught with a similar rig and bait as used to catch yellowtail and cowanyoung. Most fish caught are about 18 cm (7 in) long.

YELLOWTAIL
Trachurus novaezelandiae

Also known as Yakka, or Scad.

The yellowtail is our most common baitfish. It is often referred to as scad or yakka and confused with cowanyoung, a close relative. Colouring is very similar, yellowish-green above the lateral line and silver below. It has scutes along the entire length of its body.

HABITAT AND GROWTH
The species grows to a length of 33 cm (13 in) but the average fish caught is about half that size. It is often seen feeding around jetties and wharves in the many bays and estuaries around the coast.

FISHING

They are a hardy little fish and as a live bait they excel. Use a no. 6 long-shanked hook and a light 2 kg (5 lb) nylon line with a tiny split shot about 23 cm (9 in) from the hook. A small bait of green prawn or any fish bait will be readily taken. A small piece of flesh of their own kind is excellent bait. Cast away from the boat or jetty and allow the baited hook to slowly sink. A berley mix of bread, pollard and bran will soon have them in a feeding frenzy.

CHAPTER EIGHT

Fish with a Lunate Tail

CHINAMAN FISH
Symphorus nematophorus

Also known as Thread-finned Sea Perch and Galloper.

Juvenile fish are generally green-bronze above with pink toning. All fins are reddish pink. A series of narrow blue stripes extend the length of the fish. Some of the rays of the dorsal fins extend thread-like. In maturity these threads will disappear and the body is more pinkish with dark vertical bars. Fine yellow lines run all over the head and snout.

It is known to cause ciguatera poisoning in some cases and therefore the fish should always be considered poisonous. Do not eat it.

HABITAT AND GROWTH
It is found in reef waters all along the Queensland coast of the continent and the tropical coast of Western Australia. They attain a weight of 15 kg (33 lb).

FISHING
This fish is caught when fishing for other species.

COD, CORONATION
Variola louti

Also known as Fairy Cod, Lunate-tailed Cod and Coronation Trout.

This beautifully coloured fish is predominantly red or orange with prominent spots all over the head, body and fins. Fins are a bright golden yellow on the trailing edge, tapering to a very fine extended tip. The tailfin is a crescent shape (concave).

The flesh is firm and white and it is one of our best table fish.

HABITAT AND GROWTH
Coronation cod is fairly common in the tropical north from lat. 29°S, where its habitat is the coral reefs. It grows to a length of 76 cm (30 in). The average fish caught is about 46 cm (18 in).

FISHING
It will take almost any fish bait, prawn, crab or squid. Use a

14 kg (30 lb) line, a 6/0 strong hook and rig no. 16. It will occasionally rise to a lure trolled at about 4-6 knots.

PERCH, ROSY SEA
Callanthias allporti

A brilliantly coloured and robust fish, with a rather small mouth,

large scales and a short trailing filament on the upper and lower filaments of the caudal fin. It is mainly red with golden tonings. The caudal fin is red, all other fins are orange.

The flesh is white and firm and good eating.

HABITAT AND GROWTH
This fish is found throughout the southern half of Australia where it inhabits rocky and coral outcrops. Fish to 3 kg (6 lb) are fairly common.

FISHING
Usually caught while reef fishing using bait of fish, prawn or crab. Use a 2/0 hook on a 14 kg (30 lb) line and rig no. 16.

PIGFISH, BLACK SPOT
Bodianus vulpinus

A pinkish-brown fish with a number of darker stripes running the full length of the body. The male form has a very distinctive black blotch on the dorsal fin which is a pinkish colour and extends to the tail fin. It has a moderately large mouth and thick lips. Good eating.

HABITAT AND GROWTH
This fish is restricted to New South Wales. It attains a length of 61 cm (24 in).

FISHING
A reef dweller it is caught when fishing for other species. More would be caught if small hooks were used. A snapper rig no. 16 is ideal and a 2/0 size hook.

PIGFISH, GOLDEN-SPOT
Bodianus perditio

Also known as Golden Spot, Wrasse, and Reef Parrot.

177

This is one of our most colourful fish. It is the general shape of a parrot fish and is a rich red with golden spots all over the head and body. The scales on the rear half of the fish are black-edged; the fins are tipped in golden yellow, except the dorsal, representing the first seven or eight spines, which is jet black. The fish has a golden spot half way along the body above the lateral line, from which it gets its name.

The flesh is firm and white and is highly regarded as a table fish.

HABITAT AND GROWTH
Golden-spot pigfish is a semi-tropical fish and inhabits the off-shore reefs of southern Queensland and northern New South Wales where it grows to a length of 53 cm (21 in).

FISHING
It is caught by line fishermen on the offshore reefs when fishing for reef fish in general. Not plentiful, but very highly regarded. Use a 14 kg (30 lb) nylon line with 4/0 or 5/0 heavy duty hooks and rig no. 16. It will readily take most fresh fish baits, prawn and hermit crab.

TREVALLY, GOLDEN
Gnathanodon speciosus

Young fish are bright yellow with silver tonings. They have 10 to 12 narrow dark bars running vertically over the entire fish. As they mature, the bars fade and the bright yellow becomes golden. The fins are golden. A deep, thin fish, narrowing dramatically in front of the big swallow-tail.

The flesh is firm and white and very good eating.

HABITAT AND GROWTH
The larger fish are mostly found on the deep reefs of the Great Barrier Reef. The smaller fish shoal in great numbers south in the Bundaberg area of Queensland. Also occurs north of Australia. Grows to a maximum length of 1 m (32 in).

FISHING
The fighting qualities of the golden trevally are renowned. Many fish are taken in the estuaries on lures, when a 7 kg (15 lb) line will give great sport. On the wider grounds a 23 kg (50 lb) nylon

line is necessary. A small live baitfish such as a hardyhead or cowanyoung is the best bait. Many are taken on a line with a lure trolled deep. Use a 4/0 hook with a 14 kg (30 lb) line and a strong 6/0 to 8/0 hook out wide. Use rig no. 7, 15 or 18.

WRASSE, ROSY
Pseudolabrus psittaculus

It is a brilliantly coloured reef fish, predominantly red with rather large scales. The centre of each scale has a distinguishing yellow spot. The flesh is firm but off-white and not very good eating, although some people don't mind it.

HABITAT AND GROWTH
Its habitat is the rocky shores and the shallower reefs close to the coast. The species prefers the colder water of NSW, Victoria, South Australia, and the southern half of Western Australia, and is also found in Tasmania. It grows to about 40 cm (16 in) and the average caught is about 30 cm (12 in).

FISHING
It has a rather small mouth, and a strong 1/0 hook on a 5 kg (11 lb) nylon line will suffice. Use rig no. 13. Any fish bait will do, as will prawns, cunjevoi and crab.

179

CHAPTER NINE

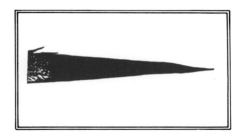

Fish with an Eel Tail Fin

CATFISH, EEL-TAIL
Neosilurus sp.

There are at least 12 different species of eel-tail catfishes, and most are very difficult to tell apart. Commonly, these fishes are dark grey with lighter mottlings on the body. The spines on the pectoral and dorsal fins can cause painful stings, so the fish should be handled with care. Named because of its distinctive tail.

Some people consider it good for eating.

HABITAT AND GROWTH
Restricted to freshwater rivers throughout inland Australia from the Murray-Darling system northwards. May reach a maximum length of almost a metre (3ft).

FISHING
Little skill is required to catch it as it will readily take most baits, including yabbies, shrimps and grubs. Use a 4 kg (9 lb) nylon line a 2/0 hook and rig no. 4.

CATFISH, LONG-TAILED
Euristhmus lepturus

Generally grey when small, but larger, more mature catfish take on a camouflage appearance with a predominance of yellow.

It has no commercial value and although the flesh is palatable, few people keep it to eat. It is a slimy fish without scales, and has fleshy whiskers around the mouth. It has poisonous spikes around the head and fins which can inflict a nasty wound that will give you hot and cold shivers for some hours. The poison is not fatal, but your interest in fishing will most certainly wane for those few hours.

HABITAT AND GROWTH
Very active around New South Wales and southern Queensland coasts, especially in the Hawkesbury River system where, after dark, it becomes a real nuisance to anglers by stealing the bait. Grows to 40 cm (16 in).

FISHING
Often caught when breaming after dark, but rarely especially sought.

EEL, PIKE
Muraenesox cinereus

Pike eels are grey on top and silvery along the sides. The dorsal fin begins at the gills and extends the full length of the body and has a black margin. Its vicious long teeth mean that care must be taken when handling.

The flesh is white and firm and edible, but rather bony.

HABITAT AND GROWTH
They grow to about 165 cm (5½ ft) and inhabit the estuaries and rivers to the brackish water zone. They seem to prefer muddy waters.

FISHING
They are not fished for but often caught when breaming and fishing for other species. They make a terrible mess of lines if landed and allowed to twist and slither about the boat. Give preference to cutting the line above the hook and give it its freedom.

GRENADIER, BLUE
Macruronus novaezelandiae

This is a bronze-blue fish with a distinct lateral line and a silvery scale portion on the lower half, it is long and tapering with a ribbon-like tail.

It is not highly regarded as a food fish.

HABITAT AND GROWTH
This grenadier is found off the coast of New South Wales, Victoria and Tasmania in depths of 20 m to 60 m (66 ft to 197 ft) where it is known to grow to 92 cm (36 in).

FISHING
They will readily take prawn, squid and most fish baits, but they are usually caught when fishing for other species and taken in trawl nets.

HAIRTAIL
Trichiurus coxii
Also known as Ribbonfish.

Hairtail is sometimes confused with a frostfish, which it closely resembles. The frostfish has a small forked tail, whereas the hairtail has a threadlike tail. It is a long silvery fish without scales. The mouth is large, with a vicious set of teeth — care must be taken when handling.

The flesh is firm and white and reasonably good eating.

HABITAT AND GROWTH
Hairtail grow to a length of about 2.2 m (7 ft 6 in) and around 5.5 kg (12 lb). The average fish is around 1.2 m (4 ft) and weighs 1 kg (2 lb). The species is plentiful off Mooloolabah, Queensland, where it is often netted when prawning. These fish always seem to be less than a metre long. Cowan, near Sydney, produces bigger hairtail all year round, especially around Coal and Candle Creek, Yeomans Bay and Jerusalem Bay. Broken Bay and Botany Bay also produce fair numbers. They enter the estuaries in late summer and autumn in the lower half of the continent, including New South Wales and Western Australia. They have not been reported in Tasmania, but could exist there.

FISHING
A live yellowtail is best, but any fish bait is acceptable. Only suf-

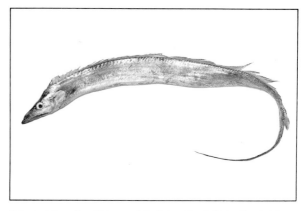

ficient sinker should be used to bring the bait to the depth at which the fish are feeding — about 6 m (20 ft) is recommended. For best results, fish a rising tide at dusk with rig no. 10 to 26 or 27.

SEA HORSE
Hippocampus whitei

An armoured fish with the body encased in a series of bony plates. The head and long tubular snout resemble those of a horse, hence the name. The fish often swims slowly in an upright position. The common sea horse is capable of fairly rapid colour changes to suit the environment. It is generally a pale gold with darker marble tones and a smattering of small dark spots.

HABITAT AND GROWTH
Found in sheltered bays and inlets close to the coast from southern Queensland down the NSW coast, Victoria and South Australia, where it grows up to 20 cm (8 in). It swims upright, propelling itself with the aid of the dorsal and pectoral fins.

FISHING
It is not fished for, but is sometimes taken by prawners in their nets near weedbeds.

MOLLUSCS, CRUSTACEANS

AND OTHER INVERTEBRATES

MOLLUSCS, CRUSTACEANS AND OTHER INVERTEBRATES

LOBSTERS, CRABS AND FRESH WATER CRAYFISH

Australia is fortunate in having relatively large stocks of lobsters, crabs and freshwater crayfish. However, large quantities of lobster tails are exported to the United States so there are only limited supplies available in Australia. For that reason, lobsters are sometimes difficult to find and are always expensive. Fortunately, some of the less familiar crustaceans, such as sand lobsters, are not exported and are often available at reasonable prices.

LOBSTER OR CRAYFISH?

The names 'lobster' and 'crayfish' are both used to describe the marine crayfish which are taken in Australian waters. Although true lobsters (large marine crayfish with a pair of large claws) are not caught commercially in Australia, marine crayfish are sold under the name of 'rock lobster'. Freshwater species are known as 'crayfish', and include marron, Murray crayfish and yabbies.

LOBSTERS AND CRABS

Four species of rock lobster are fished commercially in Australia. The most important, western rock lobster, is found in Western Australia where it supports one of Australia's richest export fisheries. The southern rock lobster is found in large numbers in South Australia, Tasmania and Victoria and is sold in local markets as well as being exported. Smaller numbers of the eastern rock lobster are taken off New South Wales. In Queensland, Northern Territory and Western Australia small numbers of the tropical rock lobster are taken. As the name implies, all these species inhabit rocky foreshores.

The rock lobster is a marine curiosity. It can shed a leg or two and its complete shell, but each grows again. It can move forward and backward because it has interlocking joints on its legs and body. It also tends to be gregarious yet at moulting time can be cannibalistic. Biologists believe rock lobsters can talk to each other by means of squeaks emitted when a pad at the base of their feelers is rubbed on a raised rim below their eyes. Experiments in Western Australia have shown that when trapped in pots they transmit panic signals to warn other lobsters of danger. This has led to a suggestion that the sound of happily eating lobsters should be recorded and played back in baited pots.

Two species of sand lobster (flat marine crayfish) are sold in eastern Australia — the Balmain bug and the Moreton Bay bug (the latter is also called bay lobster). The Moreton Bay bug is found throughout the northern half of Australia, but Balmain bugs are found only in New South Wales and Victoria. Many consumers think the two sand lobsters are the same species but you can tell them apart by the position of the eyes — the Moreton Bay bug's are on the outer edge of the head on long eyestalks, and the Balmain bug's are in the centre of the head on short eyestalks.

There are only three commercially important species of crab caught in Australia. The sand crab, which is called blue swimmer in NSW and blue manna in Western Australia, is found right around Australia, whereas the mud crab or mangrove crab, one of Australia's largest crabs, is taken in large numbers in Queensland. It is, however, widely distributed in northern Australia and parts of NSW. The third species, the spanner crab, is also taken in large numbers in northern Australia. This species has its name because its large claws look remarkably like a pair of spanners.

THE YABBIE
There are several species of freshwater crayfish in Australia but only one is sold in large numbers — the yabbie of eastern Australia. It is caught in quiet creeks, billabongs, lakes, farm dams and irrigation canals. The marron and gilgie are the freshwater crayfish commonly caught by amateur fishermen in the south-west of Western Australia. The large Murray crayfish, which has distinctive white claws and spines on its tail, is captured by amateur and commercial fishermen in the Murray and Murrumbidgee Rivers.

HANDLING LIVE CRUSTACEANS
A rock lobster may be picked up by firmly clasping it at the back of the head near the junction of the head and tail (when picked up the lobster will probably flap its tail to free itself). Sand lobsters are easy to handle because they are smaller, but they, too, may flap their tails and should therefore be gripped firmly.

Sand and mud crabs are not easy to handle unless they have been tied up beforehand. Fortunately, fishermen tie the crabs' claws soon after catching them, to facilitate marketing and handling. Nevertheless, tied crabs should be handled carefully to avoid a nasty accident. Live yabbies should be picked up at the junction of the head and tail. When held in this way the claws cannot reach back to nip your hand.

MOLLUSCS

ABALONE, BLACKLIP
Haliotis ruber

These shellfish have a flat, roughly oval shell and cling to the rocks with a large muscular foot which provides the meat for processing. The shell is red, streaked with light green and is roughly corrugated. The interior is lined with mother-of-pearl and there is a spiral row of holes around the non-growing edge of the shell. Its common name, blacklip, comes from the black mantle, a little fold of tissue that surrounds the foot of the mollusc.

The muscle is meaty and tastes good.

HABITAT AND GROWTH

Blacklip abalone is most prolific in Tasmania, Victoria and South Australia and extends into Western Australia and NSW. It inhabits crevices and caves and growth depends on geographic location and the amount of water movement. Abalone that live on coastal exposed reefs grow faster than those in sheltered conditions. Feeds at night on sea weed. Grows to a maximum diameter of 20 cm (8 in) and can produce about 560 g (1¼ lb) of clean meat.

FISHING

Abalone is caught professionally in waters near the open sea. It was plentiful just near the low tide limit but overfishing has reduced the numbers and it is not so easy today to find them in such shallow water — especially near populated areas.

Abalone should be killed with a mallet as soon as they are removed from the shell, otherwise the muscles contract and become tough, requiring tenderising with a meat mallet. Even so, a little tenderising is still necessary to break up the tissue.

Prepare for the table by cutting into thin slices after tenderising, cover in corn flour, dip into beaten egg, then breadcrumbs, and fry for only 45 seconds — in very hot oil or butter.

ABALONE, GREENLIP

Haliotis laevigata

The shell is smooth, pale, with little surface sculpture, often heavily bored by sponges and other animals, the interior is of mother-of-pearl, paler than the preceding species, but there is the same row of holes.

The shell is red, streaked with light green and is roughly corrugated. The interior is lined with mother-of-pearl and there is a spiral row of holes around the non-growing edge of the shell. Its common name, greenlip, comes from the green mantle, a little fold of tissue that surrounds the foot of the mollusc.

It is chewy meat and tastes good.

HABITAT AND GROWTH

Found along the southern continental coast of Australia from Wilson's Promontory to Cape Naturaliste. It also occurs around Flinders, Swan and King Islands in Bass Strait and along the northwest coast of Tasmania. It lives under boulders until about 12 months old and then moves to open conditions along the coast and offshore. Unlike blacklip abalone, it prefers to live on open rock faces and sea grass beds. The greenlip abalone grows to a maximum size of 22 cm (9 in) diameter and lives for about twelve years. In South Australia it reaches legal size, 10 cm (4 in) shell width, at 3 years of age.

FISHING

Greenlip abalone is caught mainly by professionals using 'hooker' gear. This abalone lives below the surface and divers prise it from open sea rock shelves with a tool similar to a chisel. Prepare for the table as described for blacklip. The flesh is off-white and the mantle should be scrubbed hard with salt to remove the green lip.

CLAM, GIANT

Tridacna spp.

There are at least five species of giant clam on the Great Barrier Reef. The largest, *Tridaena gigas*, attains a length of more than 1 m (3 ft). It is illegal to take giant clams on the Great Barrier Reef but poaching by foreign vessels is rife and is depleting our stocks. It is estimated that more than 400,000 clams were aboard 14 Taiwanese fishing vessels apprehended on the Reef. Scientists report that it takes the smallest of the species up to 40 years to reach maximum size.

Giant clams are protected and must not be taken or harmed.

COCKLE, ARK
Anadara trapesia

This cockle shell is of two similar, very solid, deep-dished shells hinged near the pointed region. The outer sculpture is heavily, vertically ridged and is generally covered with a dark brown, velvety cover. Inside, the shell is pure white.

It is good eating, especially if roasted in the shell

HABITAT AND GROWTH
Ark cockles reach about 70 mm (3 in). They can be found in dense concentrations in mud and eel grass flats in the low tidal zone in estuaries in our warmer waters from W.A. to N.S.W. and New Guinea. The animal is very characteristic in being bright red, from having haemoglobin in the blood, an unusual occurance in molluscs.

MUSSEL
Mytilus planulatus

The mussel is a bi-valve shellfish found in bays and inlets south of about 30° latitude on the Australian coast, including

Tasmania and islands in Bass Strait. The colour of the shell varies from brown to a purple-black. Good eating.

HABITAT AND GROWTH
It grows in the sheltered waters by attaching itself in clusters to permanent mooring lines, wharves and jetty piles. A very similar species commonly encrusts rock platforms along our coasts. Its shell is very much more hairy. When removed from the sea the mussel should be cooked within 24 hours. Plunge them into boiling water and the shell will open in minutes. Remove the muscle and the attaching threads from the shell. Serve with vinegar, pepper and salt.

FISHING
Prise or push from its anchorage.

OYSTER, ANGAS'S
Ostrea angasi

Native to the east coast, especially in shallow areas such as Lake Macquarie.

Not as tasty as the Sydney rock oyster when eaten raw, but popular in prepared dishes. Sometimes it has a muddy look and taste, but if it is suspended in a hessian bag in a tidal stream where it is covered for 5 to 6 hours in a tide for 3 or 4 days, the flavour is greatly enhanced.

The large Angas's Oyster photographed here with the Sydney Rock Oyster.

FISHING
A free-floating mollusc.

OYSTER, SYDNEY ROCK
Saccostrea commercialis

The cultivation of the Sydney rock oyster is a thriving industry on the east coast of Australia from Tin Can Bay on the mid-Queensland coast along the NSW coast to Mallacoota Inlet in Victoria.

The Sydney rock oyster has an international reputation for excellent taste.

HABITAT AND GROWTH

Spawning occurs chiefly during summer and it tastes best in the pre-spawning period (November-February). It spawns for the first time as a male, but changes to a female later on. Just prior to spawning it is full and creamy white in prime condition, but after spawning it becomes shrunken and watery. Growth is variable, but generally it is a marketable size in 3 years.

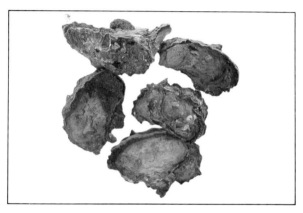

The Sydney rock oyster is able to survive in the shell and out of the water for up to two weeks. It is best stored in a damp hessian bag in a cool place. Do not put it in a plastic bag, as it will sweat and die quickly. It will also die quickly under refrigeration.

Generally, but not always the shell will gape when the oyster is dead. It must not be eaten. The law requires that bottled oysters must be packed in clean fresh water with no preservatives. In some States the bottle is required by law to carry a label with the source of supply and a recommended consumption date. Be careful if the liquid is cloudy.

FISHING

The law allows you to eat you fill from public leases, but forbids removal in the shell or as meat in a jar or other container.

PIPI

Donax deltoides
Also known as Goolwa Cockle and Ugari.

The smooth polished outer surface of the roughly triangular shell may be various shades of olive green, pink, lavender or yellow.
Good bait, but rarely eaten.

HABITAT AND GROWTH

Pipis live inter-tidally a few centimetres below the surface of the sand on shallow sloping beaches, particularly those near estuaries along exposed coasts. They maintain their position below the sand surface by burrowing with an extendable tongue-shaped flap of muscle. They are found from southern Queensland along the eastern and south-eastern coast of Australia, around Tasmania and along the south coast of South Australia.
The pipi is formed of two similar wedge-shaped shells hinged near the pointed end by a visible ligament. Large specimens attain shell lengths of more than 8 cm (3 in).

They are excellent bait and were harvested commercially with mechanical diggers for some years until their numbers depleted and it became uneconomical. Then along came the sand miners and now pipis can be found only on very isolated beaches. Fishermen played their part in depleting stocks, too, by taking far more than they needed and not returning what they didn't use to their beachside environment. There is clear evidence that beaches where they are plentiful, fish considerably better.

FISHING

They are harvested by squirming your heels in the sand as a shallow wave runs out. The movement displaces the pipi so it can be picked up off the wet sand.

SCALLOP, COMMERCIAL

Pecten fumatus

The shell of the commercial scallop is strongly ridged and its colouring may be yellow, orange, pink or brown, or a combination of all four. It is a fan-shaped shell, flat on one side and domed on the other, with radiating ridges.
The white muscle and yellow gonad are a delicacy.

HABITAT AND GROWTH

It is found in waters around the southern half of Australia, on sand or on sand silt bottom in coastal bays and in deeper water on the Continental Shelf. It propels itself by opening and closing the shell and jetting water.

FISHING

Much sought after by commercial trawlermen.

SCALLOP, SAUCER
Amusium balloti

Scallops are bi-valve molluscs but this one differs from other varieties by having a relatively smooth shell, the edges of which are very thin. Its colouring may be yellow, orange, pink or brown or a combination of all four.

The white meaty muscle has a slightly sweet flavour and is considered a delicacy.

HABITAT AND GROWTH

Found in the warmer waters from northern N.S.W. to Queensland and Shark Bay in W.A. It grows rapidly and reaches maturity within two years. Maximum size is aobut 11.5 cm (4½ in), measured from the hinge to the opposite edge of the shell. It propels itself by opening and closing the shell and jetting water.

FISHING
It is trawled commercially on a sandy bottom in only moderately deep water.

SQUID, GOULD'S

Nototodarus gouldi
Also known as Arrow Squid and Flying Squid.

It has a cylindrical body tapering to an acute point, with triangular fins extending about a quarter of the body length.
The flesh is very good table food.

HABITAT AND GROWTH
A common species of squid found in southern Australian waters from Western Australia to NSW. Occurs in estuaries and bays where it grows to 1.5 kg (3¼ lb) and 76 cm (30 in) but is mainly caught commercially by jigging over deeper water on the Continental Shelf.

FISHING
Squid can be enticed to the surface with a strong light at night where they can be taken with a spear or netted. To prepare for the table, the soft bone (pen) is removed with the head, the body slit and thoroughly washed. It is then cut into thin slices (about 6 mm (¼ in) wide) and dipped into cornflour, beaten egg, breadcrumbs and deep fried for no more than 40 seconds.

SQUID, SOUTHERN CALAMARI

Sepioteuthis australis

Fins are broad and extend full length of the mantle. Body is cylindrical, bluntly pointed at the rear.

They are very good eating. To prepare for the table, remove the soft bone, the tentacles and the ink bag. Wash squid and tentacles well to remove sand and mucus. Slice the meat into

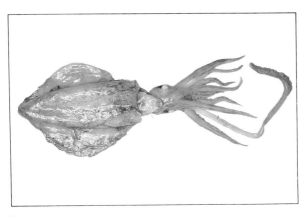

fingers about 6 mm (¼ in) wide. Dust with cornflour, dip into beaten egg and deep fry for a few minutes.

HABITAT AND GROWTH
They are found from Torres Strait around the eastern and southern Australian coastline to Western Australia. Maximum length is about 90 cm (35 in) and weight is about 1.6 kg (3½ lb).

FISHING
Generally caught commercially. Occasionally they will attack a hooked fish and hold on with their sucker-armed tentacles, tearing at the flesh with a parrot-like beak. When alongside they can be netted but you have to be quick.

CRUSTACEANS
CRABS

CRAB, BLUE SWIMMER
Portunus pelagicus
Also known as Blue Manna and Sand Crab.

♂ D

♂ V

♀ D

♀ V

As the name suggests, the blue swimmer crab is blue on top and white below. It has two paddles on its rear legs which are used for swimming. The male has much longer nippers than the female and is a deeper blue. The underside flap of the male is tapered, whereas the flap on the female is square. Females should be allowed to go free for breeding stock.

Very good eating.

HABITAT AND GROWTH

This species of sand crab is plentiful throughout Australian waterways, preferring shallower waters in estuaries and up to 40 m (45 yds) offshore. It attains a shell width of up to 20 cm (8 in) and a weight of 1 kg (2 lb).

FISHING

It may be caught in a trap known as a witch's hat. This is a cone-shaped net about 1 m (3 ft) in diameter at the base and 1 m (3 ft) high, to which a small float is attached so the net will keep its

The female Blue Swimmer in berry. Females in this condition should be released.

shape. Bait is suspended inside the net and when the crab tries to get at it, it becomes entangled. The net is best left overnight and retrieved in the morning.

Crabs shed their shells regularly. To handle, hold the nippers closed in your hand. The crab will die within hours of being caught and must be cooked soon after catching.

Boiling: A large crab requires about 15 minutes on the boil in salted water.

Steaming: A large crab requires about 10 minutes.

To clean and prepare for the table: Lift the under flap with your thumb and the whole shell will come away. Pull away the furry bits, clean and break into portions for the table.

CRAB, CORAL

Charybdis cruciata

The coral crab is similar in shape to a blue swimmer crab with distinctive reddish stripes across a creamy body. It has a relatively smooth shell without spines at the edges. The legs and claws are mottled reddish-brown and white.

It is a good eating crab.

HABITAT AND GROWTH

As the name suggests is it a coral species that grows to a width of 17 cm (6¾ in).

CRAB, GIANT TASMANIAN
Pseudocarinus gigas

This giant is the largest of all Australian crabs and second in size only to the giant king crab found off Japan. It has a white shell and the claws are splashed with red. Good to eat.

HABITAT AND GROWTH
It is reasonably plentiful between 90 and 150 m (50-80 fathoms) in Bass Strait and off the eastern coast of Tasmania. It can weigh over 13 kg (29 lb) and measure 36 cm (14 in) across the body and have arms with giant pincers around 46 cm (18 in) long.

FISHING
Generally caught commercially.

CRAB, HERMIT
Famiiy *Paguridae*

The tail of the hermit crab is soft and about as long and as thick as an adult's index finger. The body, limbs and nippers are a deep red — which is all you can see of the crab once it crawls inside its chosen shell. When it outgrows a shell it must make a hasty move, as it will easily fall prey to any number of inhabitants of the deep. Once inside the new shell, it is protected by an extra long claw that closes the entrance.

Not table fare.

HABITAT AND GROWTH
It ranges all around the Australian offshore reefs and shoals. A fully matured crab can measure about 25 cm (10 in) long.

FISHING
It is caught offshore in craypots and by trawler fishermen. Not

an edible crab, it is sold for bait, a use for which it has no peer. Only the soft tail is used.

CRAB, MUD

Scylla serrata

Often referred to as a Mangrove or Muddy Crab.

Found in NSW, Queensland, Northern Territory and Western Australia. It has great power in its huge nippers and even though fishermen tie them up soon after catching, treat them with respect. It is an offence to keep the female, which is easily distinguished by the 'flap' on the underside. The female, called a jenny, has a square-shaped flap whereas the flap of the male is tapered. They have a remarkable ability to 'throw' a claw, after which they retire from the battle scene and eventually grow a new one. It is possible to catch a crab with one full claw and one only half size. It isn't deformed, merely in the process of growing.

Delicious eating.

HABITAT AND GROWTH
It lives in mud flats and tidal estuaries, particularly mangrove-lined shores. Body colour varies from greenish-brown to brownish-blue marked with purple. In southern Queensland it reaches legal size, 15 cm (6 in) carapace width in the third year from the egg.

FISHING
Mud crabs are caught commercially by positioning pots along the mangrove creeks. The pots are a simple wire netting cage

with a funnel-shaped entrance at one end and a door at the top through which the crabs are retrieved. A bait is suspended in the cage.

Another way of catching them is to use a bait-filled 'dilly-bag'. This is a round net about 1 m (3 ft) in diameter onto which the bait is fixed. The net is attached to a steel rod with lines leading to a ring with another line attached to a float on the surface. They should be carefully hauled to the surface every half hour.

CRAB, RED-SPOT

Portunus sanguinolentus

Closely related to the blue swimmer crab and very similar in shape and size. However the body is a blue-grey colour with three distinctive red spots on the shell. The tips of the claws are red.

It is a good eating crab.

HABITAT AND GROWTH

Found along the far north coast of New South Wales and southern Queensland including Moreton Bay these crabs attain a shell width of 18 cm (7 in).

CRAB, SOLDIER
Mictyris longicarpus

Bright blue, yellow and purple, the soldier crab is a little dome on legs.

HABITAT AND GROWTH
Prevalent on sandy spits in estuaries, the soldier crab is found in large colonies, and is usually up and feeding when the tide exposes the spit it inhabits. It is not aggressive and when disturbed burrows quickly into the sand. It has nippers, but

generally if you pick one up it will curl itself into a ball and stay still. It grows to only about 2½ cm (1 in) in diameter.

FISHING
Three or four of these crabs on a hook make an excellent bait for black bream and whiting.

CRAYFISH

CRAYFISH, MURRAY
Euastacus armatus

The claws and the body spines are white-tipped and the body and head are dark blue. Like the saltwater lobster it resembles, it is highly prized and much sought-after.

HABITAT AND GROWTH
It lives in running rivers and streams but can survive for some weeks in drought periods when the rivers dry up. Body length is about 30 cm (12 in) and weight up to 1 kg (2 lb).

FISHING
Caught commercially in the Murray and Murrumbidgee Rivers with a wire mesh trap. When the streams are clear, Murray crayfish can often be seen on the bottom and amateurs coax them up with meat or fish on a line to within reach of a landing net.

MARRON
Cherax tenuimanus

Marron were once confined to the larger permanent freshwater pools of coastal streams in the south-west of Western Australia between Perth and Albany. The introduction to man-made water storage systems has expanded their distribution considerably. They do not, however, have the ability to survive the occasional summer disappearance of pools as can other native species.

Marron are held in very high esteem as a gourmet food and all wild stock are protected by law from commercial exploitation.

HABITAT AND GROWTH
A pair of median spines on the central tail fan separates marron from other native freshwater crayfish. It grows to a maximum size of about 2 kg (4 lb). The tail constitutes 42 per cent of its total body weight, and the claws an additional 19 per cent. During daylight it rests in the deep holes under fallen debris or trees for shelter from predators. At sunset it moves out to forage for food.

FISHING

Marron is coaxed to the surface with a piece of fresh meat or fish on a line and netted with a hand-held net.

YABBIE, FRESHWATER

Chaerax destructor

There are several species of freshwater crayfish in Australia, of which the yabbie is one. It is about the size of a king prawn and the shape of a lobster with claws.

The flesh is good eating but should be well salted.

HABITAT AND GROWTH

It grows to a length of 15 cm (6 in). It hibernates in burrows from June to September and then emerges to spawn, and sheds its shell for a growth period. It is found in large numbers in freshwater dams, lakes and creeks west of the Great Dividing Range and in South Australia.

FISHING

Excellent bait for Murray cod and golden perch, they are caught by attaching a number of lines about 2-3 m (6½-10 ft) long, to a pole. Each line is baited with a piece of raw red meat. When you see the yabbie feeding, haul in the line and grasp the whiskers as they break the surface.

YABBY, SALTWATER

Callianassa australiensis

A yabby is a prawn-like crustacean. It has one enormous claw which is smaller in the female.

HABITAT AND GROWTH

Yabbies feed on organic matter strained from the sand. They burrow up to 61 cm (24 in) in estuaries.

FISHING

A yabby makes excellent bait for bream and in fact most fish. They are gathered with a yabby pump, (explained under equipment). To keep them alive, keep in a bucket in the shade and replace the water at frequent intervals.

205

LOBSTERS

BUG, BALMAIN
Ibacus

This flat marine lobster resembles the bay lobster or Moreton Bay bug. The eyes of the Moreton Bay species are on the outer edge of the head, but the eyes of the Balmain bug are on short eyestalks in the centre of the head. They are both sand lobsters. Good eating.

HABITAT AND GROWTH
It is found only in NSW and Victoria. Although sold in reasonable quantities, the name certainly does little to encourage buyers. It attains a length of 25 cm (10 in).

FISHING
Usually netted professionally by otter trawlers.

FLAPJACK
Scyllarides squammosus

This lobster is easily identified by its unusual wedge shape and its distinct brown-red colouring. It lacks the antenna found on the common and coral crayfish. The shell is very rough.

It is very good eating.

HABITAT AND GROWTH
It is found in waters of southern Queensland from about the Whitsundays down, where it grows to attain a length of about 26 cm (10 in).

LOBSTER, BAY
Thenus orientalis

Also widely known as Moreton Bay bug, by which name it is sold. It is yellowish with brown spots all over, except the tail fan, which is a golden shade. It is similar in size and colouring to a Balmain bug, except the eyes of the bay lobster are on the outer

edge of the head, instead of on short stalks in the centre of the head, as they are on the Balmain bug.

It has good local potential, although the name 'bug' could not help sales. The flesh of this flat crustacean is like that of a lobster.

HABITAT AND GROWTH
It ranges the entire northern half of Australia from Moreton Bay in Queensland to Exmouth Gulf in Western Australia. It attains a length of 25 cm (10 in) and a weight of about 250 g (8½ oz).

FISHING
It is caught by commercial fishermen trawling for prawns.

LOBSTER, EASTERN ROCK

Jasus verreauxii

Eastern rock lobster is olive green and lacks the many spines associated with rock species.

When cooked it is orange, and tasty.

HABITAT AND GROWTH
Found only along the coast of NSW where specimens 92 cm (3 ft) long and weighing 8 kg (17 lb) have been taken. This measurement excludes the antenna. The width at the widest part of the body can be 28 cm (11 in). The average size is 2-3 kg (4-7 lb).

FISHING
Caught in cray pots on the Continental Shelf generally close inshore. Amateurs are allowed to use two pots but they must be clearly marked with the owner's name and address on the float.

LOBSTER, SOUTHERN ROCK

Jasus novaehollandiae

Body colour varies but is more usually reddish-purple and orange in shallow water, changing to purple and creamy yellow with depth. Females can be recognised by two small reproductive

apertures at the base of the third pair of walking legs, and the last leg has a small pincer in addition to a claw at the tip. Males also have two reproductive apertures, but these are at the base of the last pair of walking legs. Excellent to eat.

HABITAT AND GROWTH
Southern rock lobsters range in colder waters off the southern coast of Australia and Tasmania where they grow to a body-length of 16 cm (6¼ in) and a weight of 4 kg (9 lb). Females grow more slowly and attain a weight of only 2 kg (4 lb).

FISHING
They are the subject of a big industry. Fishing for them, and their behaviour, is closely monitored by Parks and Wildlife and Goverment fishing authorities.

It is illegal to take females in berry at any time and there is a closed season.

LOBSTER, TROPICAL ROCK
Panulirus ornatus
Because of its multi colours it is often referred to as the Painted Lobster.

Good eating.

HABITAT AND GROWTH

This species is found off Queensland, the Northern Territory, Torres Strait Islands and the tropical coast of Western Australia. It lives in the coral areas and although fairly plentiful is not fished commercially in any great numbers, but fetches a big price at market. It inhabits coral reef crevices, usually at a depth below 15 m (50 ft) but is known to move into shallow water. Unlike other lobsters it does not enter baited pots.

FISHING

Numerous methods are used to chase tropical rock lobsters from under reefs and crevices. The most popular is to thrust a teased rope wrapped around a spear under the coral and as the lobster darts from the reef it is speared or netted.

Five species of tropical rock lobster have been recorded in northern Australian waters but only one, *Panulirus ornatus,* is caught in commercial quantities.

LOBSTER, WESTERN ROCK
Panulirus longipes cygnus

Normal colour is red but this can range from dark pink to deep maroon. When very young and moulting they are a very light pink. Females can be recognised by two small reproductive apertures at the base of the third pair of walking legs. The last (5th) leg has a pincer in addition to a claw at the tip. The males do not have this pincer. Males have two reproductive apertures at the base of the last pair of walking legs.

Excellent table quality.

HABITAT AND GROWTH

Western rock lobsters are found between Exmouth Gulf and Cape Naturaliste in Western Australia and are the source of a very big industry. They are found on reefs to the edge of the Continental Shelf where they can attain a carapace body-length of 15 cm (6 in) and a maximum weight of 2.6 kg (5 lb). Females carry their eggs for four to eight weeks externally under the abdomen. The larvae hatched from the eggs float to the surface and with the aid of wind and currents drift up to 500 km from the coast. After about 11 months the larvae drift back to the inshore reefs and five years later reach maturity.

FISHING

It is illegal to take a female in berry (with eggs).

PRAWNS

PRAWN, BANANA
Penaeus merguiensis

The head spike of the banana prawn is very long in juveniles, but becomes smaller in relation to overall length as it grows older. In

adults, the spike has a high triangular blade. Body colour is generally cream to yellow, sometimes with a reddish tinge.

Banana prawns make very good eating and are exported in large quantities.

HABITAT AND GROWTH
This species lives throughout the Indo-Pacific region from about 67° to 166°E longitude and from 25°N to 29°S latitude. Adults are rarely found in water deeper than 40 metres.

The banana prawns form large schools, and catches of up to 27,000 kg (60,000 lb) a day have been made. It is fished mainly in the Gulf of Carpentaria and Joseph Bonaparte Gulf, with some catches as far south as Nickol Bay in Western Australia.

The male is smaller than the female. Males have a carapace length of up to 42 mm (1 ⅝ in) and a weight of about 49 g (1 ¾ oz); females up to 45 mm (1 ¾ in), and 60 g (2 oz).

FISHING
Netted commercially in deep water.

PRAWN, BROWN TIGER
Penaeus esculentus

As their name implies, brown tiger prawns are striped with alternate bands of black and dark brown or yellow and rusty orange. The whiskers are striped brown and white. The walking legs are also striped and the bases of the swimming legs are yellow. These prawns are good to eat.

211

HABITAT AND GROWTH

These prawns are found in warmer waters around the northern coast of the continent from Sydney to Shark Bay, Western Australia. Adults are caught offshore in depths between 15 m and 200 m (16-220 yds). Juveniles live in estuaries. Males reach a carapace length of 52 mm (2 in) and a weight of 58 g (2 oz). Females reach a carapace length of 55 mm (2¼ in), which is equivalent to a total length of about 25 cm (10 in) and a weight of 105 g (3¼ oz).

FISHING

Brown tiger prawns are generally caught at night, while at times during daylight when conditions are favourable they can sometimes be taken in large quantities.

PRAWN, EASTERN KING

Penaeus plebejus

Eastern king prawns are grooved prawns — they have a pair of parallel grooves running the length of the upper surface of the carapace. The body is cream to yellow. The head grooves are brown and there are short brown stripes on the sides of the tail

segments. The tips of the tailfans are blue and the walking legs are yellow.

Large king prawns are generally exported frozen, green and beheaded; small to medium ones are sold in Australia cooked whole.

HABITAT AND GROWTH

Eastern king prawns are found along the eastern coast of Australia from Lakes Entrance in Victoria to North Reef in Queensland. They are caught as juveniles in estuaries during spring and summer and as adults on the Continental Shelf at depths of 60 to 220 m (200 to 725 ft) from mid-summer through winter. Normally, male eastern king prawns grow to a length of 19 cm (7½ in) and weigh 110 g (4 oz). Females can grow to 30 cm (12 in), and weigh 220 g (8 oz). Besides being smaller, males can be distinguished by a petasma (genital appendage) between the first pair of swimming legs. Females have a plate-like thelycum at the base of the last pair of walking legs.

FISHING

Caught by deep sea netting, or in estuaries by a hand-held net wielded by a wading person using a bright light to attract the juveniles.

PRAWN, GREENTAIL
Metapenaeus bennettae
Also known as the Greasy Back.

This almost transparent prawn is speckled with olive brown, with a green tailfan. The shell is covered with fine hairs, which feel greasy when they are rubbed, hence the name 'greasy back'.

Greentail prawns make good eating.

HABITAT AND GROWTH

This prawn is found along the eastern coast of Australia from Coila Lake, NSW, to Cooktown in Queensland. The adult prawns are found in estuaries during the spring and summer and out to sea to a depth of 14 m (46 ft). During summer and autumn, these prawns are one of the few penaeids that can reach sexual maturity and complete their life-cycle in brackish water without entering the open sea.

Males grow to a carapace length of 20 mm (¾ in) which is an equivalent of a total length of 9 cm (3½ in). Females grow to a carapace length of 25 mm (1 in), which is an equivalent of a total length of 11 cm (4½ in).

FISHING
Netted by hand-held nets in shallow water, usually by wading people using bright lights to attract the prawns.

PRAWN, KILLER

Squilla raphidea
Also known as Mantis Shrimp.

A small crustacean basically the colour of a king prawn with a pair of claws.
Killer prawns are edible.

HABITAT AND GROWTH
This is a large species of the mantis family attaining a length of 25 cm (10 in). It is never especially fished for but caught by prawn trawlers and often finds its way amongst the catch to the fish shop.

PRAWN, PANDA

Penaeus semisulcatus

Also known as Leader, Grooved Tiger and Blue Tiger.

This is a very large prawn with tiger patterned stripes and a blue tailfan.

HABITAT AND GROWTH
The panda prawn is caught in the tropical north in small quantities. It can attain a length of 28 cm (11 in).

FISHING
Usually fished for commercially.

PRAWN, RAINBOW

Parapenaeopsis sculptilis
Also known as Coral Prawn.

It is a medium-sized prawn with four pale cross bands evenly spaced along the head and tail. Delicious to eat.

HABITAT AND GROWTH
It is trawled in small quantities along the Queensland coast and in the Gulf. It attains a length of 15 cm (6 in).

PRAWN, RED SPOT KING

Penaeus longistylus

It possesses a conspicuous red spot on the side of the body. Excellent eating.

HABITAT AND GROWTH
It is found in the tropical waters north where it is occasionally taken by prawn trawlers in limited quantity.

215

PRAWN, ROYAL RED
Hymenopenaeus sibogae

A medium-sized prawn, soft in texture. It looks stale shortly after capture. Royal red prawn is a soft prawn and is not readily acceptable to the local market where there is an abundance of other varieties of firmer flesh. However, it is being sold in increasing quantities and is often sold retail in a raw, green, peeled state.

It is good eating.

HABITAT AND GROWTH
Found in waters beyond the Continental Shelf in depths usually beyond 400 m and up to 700 m (1300 to 2300 ft) off the coast of NSW. It may well range further, but little is known about it. Fisheries research officers discovered its existence only about 1970.

FISHING
Commercially netted offshore in deep water.

PRAWN, SCHOOL
Metapenaeus macleayi

The school prawn has a smooth, translucent shell and the tips of the tailfan are blue. The central portion of the tailfan bears four large lateral spines. The front of the rostrum (head spike) curves upward and is without teeth on its upper edge. Good to eat.

HABITAT AND GROWTH
This prawn is endemic to the eastern coast of Australia between north-eastern Victoria and the Mary River, Hervey Bay in Queensland. The adults are seldom found beyond depths of 35 fathoms. Male school prawns grow to a total length of 13 cm (5 in) and females to a total length of 17 cm (6½ in).

FISHING
School prawns are generally caught during the summer and autumn and, as their name implies, often form schools, particularly in turbid waters over a muddy bottom.

PRAWN, WESTERN KING
Penaeus latisulcatus
This has a number of common names, but in Australia we know it as Western King Prawn and sometimes Blue Leg Prawn.

It is similar in general appearance to the eastern king prawn, except that its walking legs are blue and the tail fans are tipped with dark blue. Excellent table quality.

HABITAT AND GROWTH
Distributed throughout the Indo-Pacific region from the Red Sea through the Indonesian Archipelago to Japan and Korea. The western king prawn reaches a maximum length of about 26 cm (10 in). It also occurs to the west of Kangaroo Island in South Australia, around the coast of Western Australia, Northern Territory and along the Gulf of Carpentaria coast of Queensland to Thursday Island. Scattered catches have been made as far south as the Queensland-NSW border.

217

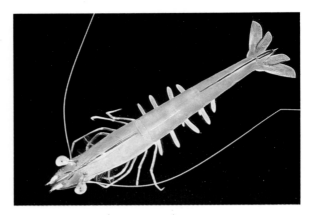

FISHING
Deep water methods as for eastern king prawn.

OTHER INVERTEBRATES

CUNJEVOI

That is an Aboriginal word for this rock dweller, a sea squirt, which is common on our rocky seashores. Over the years the name has been shortened to cunje. It is probably the most popular bait used by rock fishermen on the east coast.

HABITAT AND GROWTH
It is exposed at low tide and is a rough-looking growth firmly attached to the rock. When touched it squirts water upwards, hence its common name of sea squirt. It is entirely covered by a tough muscle. Inside it has a bag with two teats into which seawater is sucked. On first hatching from an egg, it resembles a small tadpole. After a short free-swimming life it settles and

cements its head firmly on a rock where it remains for the rest of its life.

FISHING

Cunje is gathered and prepared as bait by first removing it from the rock by cutting with a knife close to the base. This is done at low tide but as there is danger of being caught by the sea, take good care and plan your retreat. Take the cunje to safe high ground and cut the top third off. Inside you will find the two teats and hard surrounding muscle which is the toughest and therefore the best part to use. The other part can be used, but it is soft and easily stolen by small fish.

SEA WASP (BOX JELLYFISH)

This box-shaped jellyfish is prevalent along the north Queensland coast from October to March. It is one of the most feared creatures along the coast. Its jelly-type body floats with the currents, but is also capable of propelling itself at 2 to 3 knots and if alarmed can attain 5 knots. The tentacles that hang like pieces of string carry poison; a touch from them on the arm, leg or body causes severe pain to a person, and total entanglement causes death within minutes.

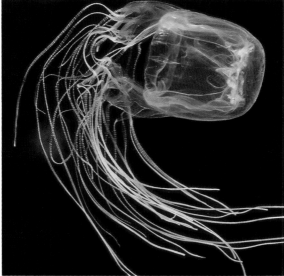

It tends to be close to shore during the summer when the northerly winds prevail and if you go swimming you should be careful and wear protective clothing. Lifesavers wear panty hose and a skivvy, a combination they find effective.

A victim should be given mouth-to-mouth resuscitation while being taken to hospital. As a temporary measure, acetic acid, vinegar or methylated spirits can be applied to the sting.

FISH INDEX

MOLLUSCS, CRUSTACEANS, ETC